S7B195
1970

2

8 1994

C

Indians of the Southwest

About the Book

It was some 30,000 years ago that the ancestors of the Indians of the Southwest migrated to the New World from Siberia. They settled eventually in the desert regions where their descendants—among them the Navajo, Pueblo, and Mohave Indians—live today. The Indians of the Southwest survived the intrusion first of the Spaniards in search of gold and later of American settlers in search of lands. In time they became the most populous of American Indian tribes. Author Gordon Baldwin tells the dramatic and exciting story of these first Americans who have successfully retained the essences of their native cultures to the present.

WILLIAM K. POWERS

Consulting Editor

AMERICAN INDIANS THEN AND NOW

Indians
OF THE
Southwest

Gordon C. Baldwin

An American Indians Then & Now Book

Earl Schenck Miers, General Editor

G. P. Putnam's Sons New York

BOOKS BY GORDON C. BALDWIN

America's Buried Past
The World of Prehistory
The Ancient Ones
Stone Age Peoples Today
The Riddle of the Past
The Warrior Apaches
Race Against Time
Strange Peoples and Stranger Customs
How Indians Really Lived
Calendars to the Past
Games of the American Indian
Talking Drums to Written Word

To my two great sons-in-law,
Alan Hutchings and Curtis Clarkson

Contents

Acknowledgments

I wish to express my thanks and appreciation to the following individuals and institutions for their cooperation in providing many of the illustrations for this book:

Dr. Robert Pennington of the Bureau of Indian Affairs; Dr. Bernard Fontana and Wilma Kaemlein of the Arizona State Museum; Dr. H. Thomas Cain, Director of the Heard Museum of Anthropology and Primitive Art; Mrs. Margaret Blaker of the Smithsonian Institution; Tad Nichols; David Brugge of the Navajo Tribal Museum; Chester Thomas and Al Schroeder of the National Park Service.

I also owe thanks to David Brugge of the Navajo Tribal Museum for information on the Navaho; to Dr. Bernard Fontana for information on the Papago and on Southwestern Indian populations; to Dr. William Kelly of the Bureau of Ethnic Research for material on the Indians of Arizona; to Tom Bahti for information on Indian arts and crafts; to Dale S. King for the loan of books on Southwestern Indians; to Dr. Robert Pennington of the Bureau of Indian Affairs for material on the Yavapai, Mescalero Apache, and Jicarilla Apache tribes; to Art Thomas for information on National Parks and Monuments; and to Dr. H. Thomas Cain of the Heard Museum for material on Pima basketry and Navaho weaving.

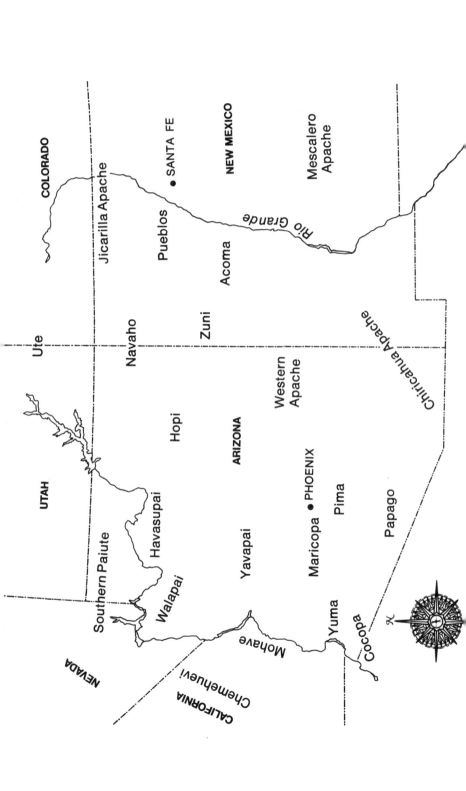

1

Introduction

BATWOMAN HOUSE, Buzzard House, Scaffold House, Cliff Palace, Hoot Owl House, Mummy Cave, Calamity Cave, Mug House, Square Tower House, Aztec, Montezuma's Castle, Pueblo Grande, Antelope House, Ladder House, Kinishba (Brown House), Snaketown, Swallow's Nest, Balcony House, Pueblo Bonito, Chettro Kettle, Betatakin (Side Hill House), Badger House, Two Raven House, Long House.

You might have a difficult time locating any of these places on an Arizona or New Mexico or Colorado road map. But they are all there. Or perhaps we should say that they were once there. Seven or eight hundred years ago these and a thousand more just like them were all thriving, populous villages and towns. Today they lie in ruins, their walls tumbled down, their plazas and courtyards deserted, their fields once green with corn and beans and squash now covered with wind-blown sand and an occasional bush or weed.

But the people who used to live in these cliff dwellings and plateau and valley villages didn't disappear into thin air. Their descendants still live not too far away in similar stone and adobe walled villages.

The dramatic and exciting story of these first Americans and their neighboring relatives is the theme of our book—the Indians of the southwestern United States.

But before we tell you about these Indians and their ways of life, let's take a quick look at the background—the country itself and its plant and animal life.

For even more than we do today, the Indians had to depend upon the resources of the area—the land and its rocks and trees and other plants and birds and animals. They made use of a great number of plants, particularly as food and also as materials for houses and utensils and tools. And they hunted birds and animals, from the largest to the smallest, both for food and for their feathers or their skins.

First, however, we'd better define the term "Southwest," as it can mean different things to different people. When we speak of the Southwest, we mean, like the archaeologist or anthropologist, the region extending from central Utah and southwestern Colorado southward through Arizona and New Mexico to the northern Mexican states of Sonora and Chihuahua and from the Pecos River in eastern New Mexico westward to and slightly beyond the Colorado River into southeastern Nevada and California.

Geographers and geologists divide the Southwest into three major physiographic divisions—mountain, plateau, and desert. Slanting diagonally from northwest to southeast across central Arizona and southwestern New Mexico is a belt of heavily timbered mountains and valleys, ending to the south in a raggedly indented line

Prehistoric cliff dwelling at Montezuma Castle National Monument, Arizona.

of cliffs ranging from a few hundred to more than 1,500 feet in height. The central section of these cliffs is known as the Mogollon Rim, named for Don Juan de Ignacio Flores de Mogollon, captain general of New Mexico from 1712 to 1715. To the north is the Colorado Plateau, high country, rough and rugged, chopped up by deep canyons and studded with sheer sides, flat-topped hills which we call mesas (from a Spanish word meaning table). Scattered throughout the southern half of the plateau are widespread lava flows, along with cinder and lava cones and extinct volcanic craters. South and west of the Mogollon Rim lies desert country, with numerous rocky mountain ranges separated by broad sandy valleys.

To the east, we might call the plains of eastern New Mexico, the western fringe of the high, grassy plains fronting the Rocky Mountains from Montana and North Dakota southward to Mexico, a fourth physiographic region.

This is a distinctive land, a unique land, a land of contrasts. There is no other region quite like it. It is big country, up and down and even sideways. Here is the world's greatest canyon, the mile-deep Grand Canyon of the Colorado River, the world's largest meteor crater, just east of Flagstaff, Arizona, the world-famous Petrified Forest, graveyard of giant trees transformed by time into rainbow-hued stone, the equally famed Painted Desert, and North America's oldest and youngest rocks. Along its western border are the world's oldest living trees, ancient bristlecone pines that began growing over forty-six hundred years ago.

This is a land of color, of amazing pinks and reds and magentas and browns and grays and buffs and yellows and greens. Over all, white sunlight beats down from a brilliant turquoise sky.

The Southwest is also a dry land, a land of little water and less rain, of rivers that often contain more sand than water, of other rivers that run underground. Real rivers are few, the Colorado River to the west and the Rio Grande to the east being by far the largest. Many of the

12

Sunset Crater near Flagstaff, Arizona.
(National Park Service)

other so-called rivers and streams are only filled with water after summer thunderstorms and midwinter rains. The rest of the year they are usually dusty and dry.

For most of the Southwest, rainfall comes in two well-defined seasons: local, frequently intense, summer thunderstorms and winter's milder storms which bring snow to the mountains and rain elsewhere. During the rest of the year anything more than a light shower is rare.

Without water, no plant or animal, including man, can exist. As a rule, the more water there is, the more abundant the plant and animal life. In the Southwest, rainfall and altitude are father and mother to the environment. As they vary, so do the climate and the plants and animals. That's why we see lots of grass and bushes and big trees in the higher mountains and few, if any, in the lower desert country.

Yet we can't actually call the desert barren. Even with its scanty rainfall, the desert can boast of a dozen or two different varieties of cactus, along with creosote bushes and widely scattered century plants (mescal) and sotol plants and clumps of grass. Nor is the desert lacking in forests. Along arroyos and washes and other areas where there is underground water, mesquite trees grow in dense thickets. So do giant sahuaro cacti and catclaw and paloverde and ironwood and Joshua trees. But you want to watch your step around these desert forests. Like the cacti, all of these trees have more than their share of sharp thorns. Cottonwoods and desert willows, both without thorns, are also occasionally found along desert stream beds. And winter rains sometimes blanket the desert with a colorful display of poppies and lupines and other desert wild flowers.

North of the Mogollon Rim pines and firs and aspens cover the higher mountains, with pinyon and juniper trees on the lower slopes. Pinyons and junipers and scrub oak trees and rabbit brush and yucca plants also cloak the upper levels of the Colorado Plateau, with scattered cottonwoods and chokecherries in the canyons and grass and yucca and sagebrush on the mesas and in the valleys. In fact, a lot of these northern mesas and plateaus look as rocky and as sandy and nearly as dry as the southern deserts.

Perhaps because animals can move around, they aren't quite as choosy as plants in deciding where to live. Elk are the exception. They like the protection of the forests. In former days these big-antlered animals were abundant in nearly all of the higher mountains in the

14

Southwest, from Utah and Colorado south to central Arizona and New Mexico. Yet their cousin, the mule deer, can be found eating the tips of quaking aspens 9,000 feet up in the mountains or gingerly picking the fruit from between the sharp spines of a barrel cactus on a hot and dry desert flat in southern Arizona. Bighorn sheep were just as much at home in the dry, sandy washes and rocky cliffs of the desert as they were in the canyons and mountains of the northern plateau country. And every grassy mesa top or valley floor from sea level to 7,000 feet had its herds of antelope. Buffalo, more correctly called bison, roamed all over the plains east of the Rocky Mountains, and some even found their way across the mountains into western Colorado and New Mexico and eastern Utah and Arizona.

Monument Valley in northern Arizona.
(Tad Nichols)

The smallest of the Southwest's big game animals is the peccary or wild pig (also called javelina). Equipped with sharp, strong tusks, a herd of peccaries can be fierce opponents, particularly if their youngsters are threatened. These little animals, rarely weighing more than 40 to 60 pounds, live in the extreme southern desert regions of Arizona and New Mexico.

Whenever these big game animals traveled, their hereditary enemies, the meat-eating lions and wolves and bobcats and coyotes, weren't far behind. Both grizzly bears, North America's largest and most powerful of all carnivores, and black or brown bears could also be found in the mountains.

Hordes of smaller animals—jackrabbits, cottontails, beaver, muskrats, ring-tailed cats, skunks, badgers, foxes, porcupines, tree squirrels, rock squirrels, ground squirrels, packrats, prairie dogs, and mice—also ranged widely throughout the Southwest. Kangaroo or jumping rats and deer mice and grasshopper mice were especially common in the desert regions. So were beaver, looking oddly out of place along shallow cottonwood- or willow-bordered streams in the middle of the hot and dry desert.

Although you might not expect to find many birds in the Southwest, there were plenty of them: ducks, geese, quail, sage hens, grouse, pigeons, doves, buzzards and vultures, hawks, eagles, owls, and hundreds of other varieties, including perhaps the region's most interesting bird, the desert roadrunner. Wild turkeys were the biggest game birds, formerly occupying most of the country's forested areas and also extending down into the mesquite thickets lining desert watercourses.

Nor should we forget snakes and lizards, perhaps the Southwest's most noted or notorious residents. Although there are more varieties of rattlesnakes in the Southwest

Desert country of southern and central Arizona below the Mogollon Rim.

(National Park Service)

than anywhere else (sixteen different kinds in Arizona alone, including the horned rattlesnake or sidewinder), they are far outnumbered by such harmless snakes as king snakes, red racers, gopher or bull snakes, and leaf-nosed snakes. Don't ever play around with rattlesnakes. So far as we know they lack a sense of humor. And even though they carry a warning rattle on the end of their tail, they don't always sound it before they strike.

Of the Southwest's many lizards, the gila monster is probably the best known and the most colorful. This walking beaded bag is also one of the only two poison-ous lizards in the world. Yet you can hardly put it in the same class with the rattlesnake. The gila monster is

17

neither as dangerous nor as deadly. Nor is he nearly as common. And gila monsters don't grow very big, generally running from a foot to a foot and a half in length. Whereas most lizards are swift of foot, the gila monster is slow-moving and awkward. If not molested, he will tend strictly to his own business.

Unique among the Southwest's lizards are the curious little so-called horned toads. They are not, of course, toads but horned lizards. In spite of their ferocious-looking horns and spiny bodies, they are harmless creatures, eating practically nothing but ants.

This picture of the Southwest's bird and animal life is as it was a hundred or more years ago. Records of early explorers and trappers and hunters reported an amazing abundance of game birds and animals throughout the Southwest. In 1825, for example, James Ohio Pattie caught 250 beaver in two weeks on the San Francisco River along the Arizona-New Mexico border. Other trappers, including the well-known mountain man Bill Williams, found beaver equally abundant on the Gila and Salt rivers in southern Arizona. These and similar stories of the Southwest's incredible wealth of vegetation and wildlife—of flocks of birds so thick they darkened the sky, of uncounted thousands of antelope, of grass as high as a tall man's shoulder—read like fairy tales to us now.

For today the picture has changed. Herds of cattle and sheep have replaced the bands of antelope. The buffalo have vanished, as have also most of the elk and wild turkeys and sage hens and grouse. Beaver and bighorn sheep have been reduced to a fraction of their original numbers. Grizzly bears have all but disappeared from the Southwest. Rivers that once flowed the year round now briefly roar to life only during thunderstorms. What grass there is usually stands not much higher than a small midget's knee. Even the desert has been stripped of thousands of mesquite and ironwood trees for firewood and fence posts.

But we can't blame the Southwest's native inhabitants for this destruction of nature's resources. We nineteenth- and twentieth-century Americans have to take credit for the lion's share.

2

The First Settlers

In 1540 Francisco Vásquez de Coronado and his army of Spanish soldiers and Mexican Indian followers came up from Mexico hunting for the legendary "Seven Cities of Cibola." The Spanish adventurers didn't run across any treasures of gold and silver. But they did find Indians all over the Southwest.

These Indians were the first Americans. None of these peoples originated in this country. They were immigrants from Asia. Some thirty thousand years ago their ancestors migrated from Siberia to the New World. North and South America were probably the last of the world's continents to be occupied by man. At that early date the Atlantic and Pacific oceans were impassable barriers to the kinds of water transportation available at that date. But these first immigrants didn't have to swim to cross the 56 miles of open water separating Siberia and Alaska. They probably walked across on dry land.

For twenty thousand years ago the world was still in

the grip of the Ice Age. So much moisture was withdrawn from the oceans to form the massive glaciers, which were up to 2 miles in thickness, that the sea level was lowered several hundred feet. This was more than enough to make the Bering Strait a land bridge connecting the two continents.

Such big game animals as mammoth and musk-ox and bison and caribou had used this bridge to migrate from Asia to America. Perhaps these first Asian immigrants were on the trail of some of these animals when they crossed the Bering Strait and unknowingly discovered a new world. Following the game and ripening wild fruits and seeds and nuts, these New World explorers pushed their way southward along the coast and the interior river valleys. Eventually their descendants, along with the descendants of later Asian immigrants, expanded throughout North, Central, and South America.

Many of these small hunting and gathering groups reached the Southwest and the adjacent plateau and plains country as early as twelve thousand years ago.

We may have to guess about a lot of the things that these first immigrants of twenty thousand years ago saw and did on their long trek southward. But we don't have to guess about what their descendants did after they settled in the Southwest. Archaeologists have found hundreds of their campsites and have dug up many of them. The stone and bone and wooden implements and utensils that these scientists have uncovered tell them how these people lived. And if the excavators are lucky enough to find remains of burials, they can figure out what the people looked like and also tell something about their religious beliefs.

Even small pieces of wood and charcoal and fiber and bone, as well as microscopic grains of pollen, have their

Diorama of early Indian hunters attacking a mammoth in southern Arizona.

(Arizona State Museum)

stories to tell. Studied and tested by geochronologists and dendrochronologists, by geologists and paleontologists, and by paleobotanists and palynologists, these fragments tell the diggers how long ago a camp was occupied, what plants and animals lived there then, and what the climate was like. (See the Glossary on p. 179 for an explanation of geochronology and dendrochronology and other technical terms.)

Archaeologists discovered that there were at least two groups of these native Southwesterners: big game hunters in the east and south and small game hunters and seed gatherers in the west and north. Although the great ice sheets which blanketed much of North America never got this far south (in fact, ten thousand years ago they were already beginning to recede), their influence was felt all over the country.

Trees and bushes, grassy meadows and parks, swamps and lakes covered the land. Flocks of birds and herds of wild animals, some of which are now extinct, attracted wandering bands of hunters into a country far different from the Southwest we know today. Some wandered in from the Great Plains with stone-tipped spears of distinctive shape, hunting mammoth and mastodon and a form of giant bison now extinct. Others came in from the Great Basin area of California and Nevada.

These spearpoints, chipped from quartzite, chert, chalcedony, jasper, and similar materials, came in a wide variety of sizes and shapes. Some spearheads were long, others short; some were broad, others narrow; some were thick, others thin; some were grooved, others ungrooved; some were leaf-shaped, others lance-shaped or triangular. Most of these people were conservative. Big game hunters chipped their spearheads in exactly the same way as their fathers and grandfathers had done. Thus archaeologists could use the different types of spearheads to identify the various groups of prehistoric hunters. They named each of these styles of spearheads, usually after the place where it was first discovered— Clovis, Sandia, Folsom, Plainview, Agate Basin, Midland, Lake Mohave, Pinto Basin, Gypsum Cave, and a dozen others.

Each projectile point speaks its own language to the

archaeologist, telling him what group of hunters made it and how long ago it was used. In many ancient sites these stone spearheads are our only link with the past. Whatever implements and utensils of wood or fiber the people might have used have not survived the effects of time and weather.

The most famous of these stone spearheads are the Clovis and Folsom, named for two sites in New Mexico where they have been found in association with the bones of mammoth and giant bison and camels and horses. Clovis Fluted points have been dated by radiocarbon at about 9200 B.C., with Folsom points about a thousand years younger. Equally old Clovis points have also been found with mammoth remains at several sites in southern Arizona.

However, this picture soon changed as the glaciers retreated still farther to the north. The climate of the Southwest became drier and drier, the forests and lakes and swamps dwindling away and the great herds of big game animals disappearing. Some animals followed the receding ice sheets northward to a cooler and wetter country. But others, like the mammoth and mastodon and giant bison and ground sloth and horse and camel, became extinct.

Archaeologists aren't certain whether these early Indians killed off the big game animals by too much hunting or whether these animals became extinct as a result of the drying and warming of the climate at the close of the Ice Age. Probably each of them, along with such other factors as famine, disease, and plague, had a hand in the final extinction of these animals.

The Indian hunters were forced to change their mode of life from one of hunting big game to one of seed gathering and of hunting the remaining smaller animals.

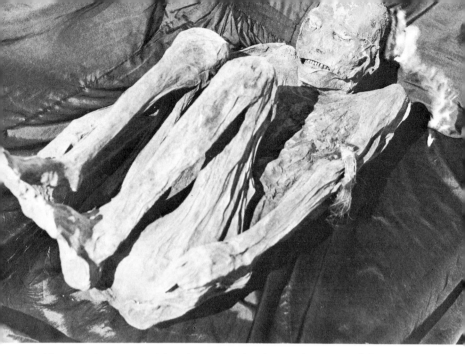

Mummy from a prehistoric cave site in northeastern Arizona.
(Arizona State Museum)

The twin markers of this new culture, which archaeologists call the Desert Culture, were the basket and the flat milling stone. The basket probably had several uses—to gather seeds and nuts and berries, to parch seeds with live coals, to store roots and nuts and other vegetable foods, and to cook soup or mush (by means of heated stones). The milling stone, as its name implies, was used to grind nuts and seeds into flour.

These Desert Indians of Utah, Nevada, California, and Arizona were foragers, utilizing everything from rats and rabbits and mountain sheep to acorns and pinyon nuts and sunflower seeds. They lived in caves when

25

they could find them—Danger and Deadman Caves in Utah, Gypsum and Fishbone Caves in Nevada, and Ventana Cave in Arizona. But most of them seem to have made their small camps out in the open.

In caves, where perishable materials have a much better chance to survive for thousands of years, archaeologists have dug up a wide variety of baskets, sandals, mats, netting, fiber bags, string, rope, buckskin, scraps of woven blankets of rabbit and bird skins, string snares and traps, wooden clubs, digging sticks, atlatls, or throwing sticks, wooden fire drills, shell beads, bone awls and needles, thousands of chipped stone dart points and knives and scrapers, and hundreds of grinding stones.

This Desert Culture seems to have been the root from which practically all of the later Southwestern cultures branched off.

One of the major roots of this Desert Culture was found down in southern Arizona and New Mexico. Archaeologists called this the Cochise Culture, naming it after the famous nineteenth-century Chiricahua Apache leader, as this was the former homeland of these Indians. But this doesn't mean that the Apaches were here seven or eight thousand years ago. The Chiricahua and other Apache tribes, as we shall see, were latecomers to the Southwest.

Like most of the other New World immigrants, the Cochise people started out as big game hunters. Their earliest campsites in southeastern Arizona are littered with the bones of mammoth, horse, and camel. But at the same time they were also gathering seeds and other wild plant foods, as the same early sites contain numerous grinding stones.

Within a thousand years or so, however, with the dying out of the mammoth and horses and camels, the Cochise people became typical Desert Culture Indians. Just like their distant cousins in Nevada and Utah, they hunted birds and small animals or fished, set out traps and deadfalls, and collected roots and berries and nuts. Within another thousand years, by about 3000 B.C. (according to radiocarbon dating), they had also become part-time farmers.

American Indian civilization is founded on a trio of agricultural products: corn, beans, and squash. (Technically, the word "maize" is preferred to the term "corn," since the latter rightly belongs to wheat and similar food grains of the Old World, but since the word "corn" has become so firmly established in our language, we will keep on using it.)

These Cochise gatherers and hunters of small game, living in the mountains of east-central Arizona and west-central New Mexico were the first Southwestern farmers. They themselves didn't discover how to plant and harvest corn. They got the idea, along with the cultivated plant, from the south, from Mexico. Several thousand years earlier some primitive Indian genius in southern Mexico or Central America, perhaps even in northern South America (actually, botanists still aren't quite certain where corn originated), had taken a wild grass and domesticated it into the plant we know today as corn or maize. From there it had spread northward, eventually reaching the Cochise people.

In Bat Cave in western New Mexico, archaeologists found hundreds of these first Southwestern corncobs. This was a primitive type of corn, far different from the highly domesticated varieties we grow today. But it was still corn, with small cobs and equally small kernels something like popcorn, since popped corn was discovered in the cave deposits. Coming up also from Mexico at about the same time was the second of North America's dominant food plants, the squash or pumpkin.

At first the Cochise people used corn and squash only to supplement the wild plant foods they gathered and the animals they hunted. Although these new plants probably furnished a greater degree of security through the storage of surplus foods, they didn't seem to have had much effect on the mode of living. Not until the third basic food plant, the red kidney bean, also imported from Mexico, was added to the menu somewhere around 1000 to 400 B.C. and pottery was adopted from the same place about 300 B.C. did the Cochise people settle down to real village life.

Once these Indians began to do more farming and build houses and make pottery, archaeologists changed their name to Mogollon, the first of at least four major prehistoric patterns of culture that ruled the Southwest for the next two thousand years.

The Mogollon people, named after the Mogollon Rim and the Mogollon Mountains located along the Arizona-New Mexico border, continued to make and use many of the stone tools made by their ancestors, the Cochise—notched and stemmed projectile points, knives, scrapers, choppers, grinding stones, including both metates and manos and mortars and pestles, and grooved hammers or mauls. There wasn't anything fancy about these stone tools. Most of them were made just good enough to get the necessary work done.

They built round or oval semisubterranean houses with timber and dirt roofs and sloping side entrances, grouping them into small villages. There weren't too many caves in these mountains, so most early Mogollon villages were located on the outside, on high ground—

on ridges, bluffs, or terraces—perhaps for defense, perhaps because farmland in the narrow mountain valleys was too scarce to be cluttered with houses. Most Mogollon villages had one larger pithouse which apparently served as a community ceremonial or religious center. Food was stored in either bell-shaped pits dug outside the houses or in bins or subfloor pits within the house.

Their earliest pottery consisted of plain red or brown jars and bowls. Later, pots were often decorated with designs painted in red on the brown background. But most of their arts and crafts stayed comparatively simple.

Luckily for archaeologists, Bat Cave and Tularosa and Cordova caves preserved such perishable items as sandals, cradles, wooden fire drills and hearths, coiled and twined baskets, leather bags, netted carrying bags, reed flutes, wooden dice, wooden atlatls and darts, shell beads and bracelets, and a variety of wild plant foods— yucca pods, cactus fruits, black walnuts, acorns, sunflower seeds, and grass seeds.

They flexed the bodies of their dead, drawing the knees up toward the chin to make a tightly folded bundle, before placing them in round pits dug between the houses. Sometimes they would put a pot or two into the grave beside the body to serve its needs in the afterworld.

From their mountain homeland in east-central Arizona and west-central New Mexico the Mogollon people began to spread out, particularly to the north and west. They soon came into contact with other Indian groups, influencing them in a great many ways and at the same time being influenced by them. They had four things other people wanted: corn, beans, squash, and pottery.

To the west, in the valleys of the Gila and Salt rivers in the south-central Arizona desert country, lived the

Hohokam (a Pima Indian word for "the old people" or "those who have gone"). Archaeologists aren't sure about the origins of this group. Some believe that these southern Arizona desert dwellers adopted corn and pottery directly from the early Mogollon people. Others think that these western Cochise Culture people, like their eastern relatives in the Mogollon Mountains, received farming and pottery directly from Mexico. Still others hold to the theory that the Hohokam, perhaps attracted by the desert valleys, moved into the area from the south, from Mexico, bringing with them a knowledge of farming and pottery.

From excavations at the large site of Snaketown in the lower Gila Valley and at other similar sites, we know that the Hohokam, by 200–300 B.C., had progressed much farther along the road to civilization than had their Mogollon neighbors. By that early date they were building houses in square, shallow pits sunk about a foot below the surface of the desert. In these they set vertical posts which supported pole and brush roofs and slanting pole and brush sides, all plastered with clay. These houses were grouped into villages, and as among the Mogollon, some of the largest houses were probably ceremonial.

The key to living in the desert is water. The Hohokam had solved the problem by digging canals and ditches to bring water from the rivers to irrigate their fields of corn, beans, and squash.

The Hohokam were skilled workers in stone and shell. Unlike the Mogollon people, they carefully finished even the most utilitarian object, frequently ornamenting it as well. They made well-shaped metates and manos, mortars and pestles, finely polished three-quarter grooved axes, carved stone paint palettes, stone vessels with lizards and snakes and other figures carved in relief around the sides, stone beads and pendants and earplugs, and a wide variety of shell ornaments, including beads and rings and carved shell bracelets.

The Hohokam made pottery as far back as we have any record of them, undecorated bowls and jars in gray, brown, or red, and a distinctive decorated style in red on a buff background. And they made lots of it. Archaeologists at Snaketown, in one winter alone, dug up and studied over a million and a half broken pieces of pottery.

Luckily for archaeologists, pots and pans will break. Yet few things last longer than the broken pieces of a pot. Even after thousands of years of exposure to wind and weather they often look as if the pot from which they came had been broken only the day before yesterday. Because designs and vessel shapes and decorator colors change with time, these broken fragments serve as time clocks to date the houses and ruins in which they are found.

The Hohokam also manufactured by hand hundreds of small human figurines of clay, which are much like figurines made far to the south in Mexico.

Archaeologists can't tell what the Hohokam people looked like, since these people had the bad habit, from the physical anthropologist's point of view, of cremating their dead. Bodies were burned in pits, with the ashes and burned bones either left in the pit and covered over with dirt or put in a pottery vessel and buried. Frequently pottery and other objects were placed beside the ashes as grave offerings.

To the north of the Mogollon and Hohokam areas lies the third of our major southwestern cultures. This was the Anasazi (a Navaho Indian word meaning "the ancient ones"), referring to the builders of the prehistoric pueblos and cliff dwellings. Centering in the Four Corners area, where the states of Arizona, New Mexico, Utah, and Colorado come together at right angles (the only such place in the United States where four states meet), it covered most of the northern half of the Southwest, from southeastern Nevada eastward to eastern New Mexico and from the Mogollon Rim northward far up into Utah.

About the beginning of the Christian Era, possibly even a century or so earlier, groups of small game hunters and gatherers in this Four Corners country picked up the knowledge of farming, probably adopting it from the Mogollon people. Who these northerners were we don't know. Perhaps they were Desert Culture dwellers from Utah and Nevada who had migrated into the area in search of a better place to make a living. Or perhaps they were refugee Cochise-like people who had journeyed northward from the mountains into a higher and drier country where there were a lot of caves to furnish ready-made roofs over their heads. For this Four Corners country is canyon and mesa land, rough and rocky and abounding in all kinds of caves and rockshelters.

Archaeologists call these first Anasazi farmers Basket Makers because of the many finely made baskets discovered in their cave sites.

We know much more about these early Basket Makers and how they lived than we do about either the Mogollon or Hohokam. Fortunately for archaeologists, many Basket Makers either lived in caves or buried their dead in them. Sometimes they did both. The caves, being extremely dry, have carefully preserved everything left there, including the bodies of the dead. Instead

32

Examples of Basket Maker coiled baskets from northern Arizona.

(Arizona State Museum)

of decaying, the bodies just dried up, becoming natural mummies. In many, even the skin and hair and finger- and toenails are preserved. Although we call these bodies mummies, they were not artificially preserved and mummified like the Egyptian mummies you see today in museums.

The Basket Makers usually placed the bodies of their dead in round pits in the floor of caves, pits which had originally been dug for the storage of food. Multiple burials of two or three bodies were common, with one storage pit holding nineteen bodies crammed tightly together. The body was tightly flexed and wrapped in a rabbit-fur blanket or in a large woven bag, slit down one

33

side. Sandals, implements, weapons, and ornaments were usually left with it as grave offerings.

These burials also tell us that the Basket Makers were Indians, probably looking much like many of today's southwestern Indians. They were short, the men averaging about 5 feet 4 inches, the women somewhat less. Most of them had long heads, coarse, straight black hair, and brownish skins.

The burials also tell us that the men spent much more time taking care of their hair than did the women. Basket Maker men usually wore their hair long and tied up in three bobs, a small one at each side of the head and a bigger one at the back. Some men had queues, braided or wrapped with cord, hanging down the back. By way of contrast, most women's hair was hacked off two or three inches from the scalp. The explanation for this is simple. The Basket Makers used a great deal of human hair as a fiber to make woven bags and nets and strong cord. When a woman ran out of weaving material, it was probably a lot easier for her to lop off a chunk of her own hair than it would have been to try to clip a lock or two from her husband's head.

The burials also tell us something about Basket Maker clothing. One essential item of wearing apparel seems to have been a pair of sandals, vitally important for protection against rocks and cactus and other thorny bushes. You might call these open-toed sandals (actually, they were open all the way around), attached to the foot by means of cords running through heel and toe loops and tied around the ankle. Sandals were made from yucca fiber cord, with a square toe which was usually decorated with a fringe of fiber or buckskin. That sandals were an essential item may also be inferred from the fact that nearly every grave shows a new pair of sandals buried with the body.

What other clothing, if any, the Basket Makers wore is not certain. Archaeologists have found a number of examples of woven bands which may have been what are popularly called G-strings or breechcloths. But few mummies have ever been found wearing one of them. Some women did wear small aprons consisting of waist cords with attached fringes of strings of yucca fiber or cedar bark or skimpy aprons of finely woven fiber which may have served as skirts. These were even shorter than today's shortest miniskirt. Their scarcity suggests that they were not regarded as essential garments.

Clothing may have been relatively scanty in summer. But chilly nights and cool winters required something more than a string of beads around the neck and a pair of sandals on the feet. Since nearly every burial is wrapped in a blanket made of strips of rabbit fur wrapped around cords, these, along with deerskin robes, probably served as wraps and blankets for the living as well as for the dead.

Basket Maker clothing may have been on the scanty side. But they more than made up for that with ornaments and jewelry. The Basket Makers wore bone pins and feathers as hair ornaments, feather pendants, stone, bone, and seed beads made into necklaces and ear pendants, and shells imported from the Pacific coast.

Some Basket Makers lived in the open, in round to oval shallow pithouses, while others camped in caves or rock-shelters.

The Basket Makers were farmers raising corn and squash in the canyon bottoms. Like most early farmers, they didn't raise enough to live on throughout the year. Women still had to harvest wild seeds and fruits and acorns and men hunted and trapped birds and animals. They stored their corn and pinyon nuts and seeds in the

Basket Maker slab-lined pithouse excavated in cave in north-eastern Arizona.

caves in circular pits which they sometimes lined with sandstone slabs. They used flat stone metates and small hand stones or manos for grinding corn.

They used the atlatl or spear-thrower in hunting large game such as deer and mountain sheep. They also used large nets, driving rabbits or other game into them. One of these nets was 240 feet long and 3 feet wide. They also had grooved curved wooden clubs, which have been called rabbit sticks.

But their most characteristic feature, the one which gave them their name, was the making of basketry. Archaeologists have found half a dozen different kinds —small trinket baskets, shallow trays, bowl-shaped types, globular jars, carrying baskets, and water jars, the latter lined with pinyon gum pitch to make them watertight. Lacking pottery, they had to use baskets for pots and pans and storage bins. Many baskets were woven so tightly as to be waterproof. These may have been used to cook soups and stews by dropping hot stones into the liquid. Large conical baskets were used for carrying loads on the back by means of a tumpline, a woven headband fastened to the basket. Baskets were frequently decorated with designs in black or in red and black. They also made egg-shaped, twine-woven bags up to 2 feet or more in length.

The Basket Makers buried not only the bodies of their own dead but also those of their one and only domesticated animal, the dog. There were at least two distinct types of dogs, one resembling a long-haired white collie, the other a shaggy-haired black and white terrier. In a Boston dog show one of these two-thousand-year-old animals won first prize as the survivor of the oldest breed.

By A.D. 400–500 the Basket Makers had begun to make pottery, probably adopting the idea from the Mogollon area to the southeast. Basket Maker plain pottery was usually gray in color, whereas the decorated ware was a black-on-white.

With farming more firmly established, the Basket Makers began to settle down in permanent houses grouped in small to large villages. These houses were pithouses, round to oval in shape, later square to rectangular. From 10 to 20 feet in diameter and from 2 to 4 or 5 feet deep, these houses usually had a flat roof, with entrance by means of a ladder through the smoke-hole hatchway in the center of the roof.

Like other southwesterners, the Basket Makers also had separate religious or ceremonial structures, a pithouse much larger than the average dwelling.

Meanwhile, in the western Arizona desert and along the lower Colorado River below the Grand Canyon, other groups of our ancient Desert Culture peoples were also turning to farming. These groups, whom archaeologists call Patayan (named after a Walapai Indian term meaning "the ancient ones"), probably learned about agriculture and pottery from the neighboring Hohokam. Some archaeologists prefer to call this culture the Hakataya (after a Yuma word for the Colorado River). The Patayan farmed the sandy flats bordering the Colorado River. However, they also depended considerably upon gathering mesquite beans and other wild seeds and nuts and upon hunting wild game and fishing. Few remains of their houses have been found, and it is probable that they lived in brush huts. Their pottery was reddish-brown in color and was sometimes decorated with designs painted in red. Like the Hohokam, many of the Patayan people cremated their dead.

Still another group of early southwesterners was the Sinagua (named by archaeologists from the Spanish words *sin agua,* meaning "without water"). Centering in the modern town of Flagstaff, Arizona, these Sinagua Indians were farmers, living in unusually deep pithouses with long side entrances. Their early pottery was a polished brown ware, much like that of the Mogollon. But sometime between September, 1064, and June, 1065, the lives of these people was drastically changed by the eruption of a volcano known as Sunset Crater.

Dated by means of tree rings, this eruption temporarily chased the Sinagua out of the area. But what was far more important, the eruption also spread a coating of fine volcanic ash over the surrounding countryside. This proved to be so fertile that Indians from all over Arizona poured into the area to get in on the ground floor of the land boom. As a result, the Sinagua picked up a lot of new ideas from the invaders. But that story belongs to the next chapter.

3

The Southwest's Golden Age

WITH A few exceptions, by A.D. 700 all of the various inhabitants of the Southwest knew about agriculture and pottery making, lived in villages, usually made up of semisubterranean pithouses, and had some type of ceremonial meetinghouse. The exceptions may have been some Desert Culture dwellers, still living entirely by hunting and gathering, on the western and northern edges of the area and some Plains-type hunters roaming the eastern and southeastern fringes.

By this time the bow and arrow had come into the Southwest, probably from the north (as it seems to have been a late introduction from Asia by way of the Bering Strait), and the bean had also reached the Southwest, coming up from the opposite direction, however, from Mexico.

Another cultural trait that spread into the Anasazi area, probably from the Mogollon area, was artificial head deformation. This seems to have resulted from the introduction of a hard, rigid cradleboard, causing the back of a baby's skull to be flattened. This new head shape soon became the fashion. In the space of a few generations it completely changed the appearance of the Basket Makers, making their normally long and narrow skulls short and broad and flattened at the back.

Yet another item imported from the south, from either the Hohokam or the Mogollon, was cotton. About the same time, the Anasazi domesticated the turkey. This brought on a change in clothing, softer and lighter turkey feather robes replacing the earlier ones made of rabbit fur.

The Hohokam, living along the Salt and Gila and Verde and Santa Cruz rivers in southern Arizona, had developed their culture more rapidly than the Mogollon of the mountains or the Anasazi of the high plateaus. They expanded their irrigation system, digging several hundred miles of canals which carried water from the Gila and Salt rivers to the flat valley lands otherwise too dry to farm. They imported a ceremonial ball game from Mexico and built huge ball courts up to 200 or 300 feet in length. They traded for small copper bells from Mexico. Occasionally they built earthen platform mounds, miniature examples of Mexican pyramids, perhaps used for similar ceremonial purposes.

Gradually the Hohokam expanded their territory, moving northward up the Verde Valley into the Flagstaff region. So did the Mogollon, also moving northward through the mountains along the Arizona-New Mexico border. By A.D. 500, the Mogollon Culture had probably reached its peak, with the Hohokam attaining its zenith by A.D. 900. But the northerners, the Anasazi, were a lot slower getting started. By the time they began making pottery, for example, the Mogollon Culture had nearly reached its peak.

By A.D. 700 or so, with the addition of pottery, the bow and arrow, the hard cradleboard, cotton, beans, and above-ground, apartment-style stone architecture, the Basket Makers stopped being Basket Makers and became Pueblo Indians. This is a general name for those Indians in the Southwest who lived in stone buildings as opposed to the tribes living in brush or mud huts, *pueblo* being the Spanish word for "town" or "village."

From this time on the Pueblo Anasazi made rapid cultural strides. But it wasn't until about A.D. 1100 that

Prehistoric pueblo of Chettro Kettle in Chaco Canyon National Monument, New Mexico.

(National Park Service)

they reached their fullest development. However, as it reached its climax, it literally overwhelmed most of the other cultures in the Southwest.

They expanded to the south and southeast, meeting both the Hohokam and Mogollon peoples, and even sent their cultural ideas or people or both northward throughout Utah and westward into southeastern Nevada.

The two or three centuries following A.D. 1000 was the period of the famous cliff dwellings and of the terraced stone buildings or apartment houses, each a whole town in itself. With the introduction of this new style of architecture, above-ground masonry structures, the pithouse became the ceremonial center. One or more of these big circular pithouses, which we call kivas, was built in each of the villages.

Probably most people lived in small pueblos of from five to twenty or so rooms. But many of the large apartment houses had two hundred to three hundred rooms. Chaco Canyon in northwestern New Mexico (now a national monument) was the center of perhaps the largest cluster of these huge apartment houses. The largest ruined pueblo, Pueblo Bonito, contained over eight hundred well-plastered rooms arrayed in four stories. Great kivas also reached their peak here.

Some of the largest and best preserved of all the cliff dwellings can be found today in Mesa Verde National Park, in the southwestern corner of Colorado.

These various local groups or cultural subdivisions of the classic Pueblo times, the period from 1150 to 1300, share most of the basic aspects of their way of life and many detailed features. Common to all of them are settled life in large and small villages, with cultivation of corn, beans, squash, and cotton, pottery, stone and bone tools, baskets and matting, cotton fabrics and wild plant

43

textiles, sandals, use of animal skins, stone, bone, and shell ornaments, turquoise, and the importation of macaws and parrots from Mexico.

Differences appear in town or settlement patterns and details of architecture, in religious or ceremonial structures, in many features of the ceramic art (as vessel shapes and types of clays and paints and styles and colors of designs), in certain other artifactual categories, and in methods of burial of the dead.

Almost within a quarter century the Great Period ended. One center after another was abandoned, the people moving away in search of new homes. The decline may have started at Chaco Canyon as early as the late 1100's. We do not know why these people abandoned their great houses. For about a century, then, population was relatively stable except for a restless moving about by small groups. Perhaps the nomadic Navaho and Apache were beginning to make inroads on the Pueblos. Restlessness and shifting increased. Agriculture must always have been difficult in the northern part of the Pueblo country because of sparse rainfall and long, cold winters. Finally, inter-village strife and social difficulties must have played a part.

Then, in 1276, a great drought set in and lasted twenty-three years; we have a record of it in the tree rings. There were a few good years during this time, and probably some corn was raised, but not enough to support a large population.

Probably no single cause led to the abandonment of the area. Short food supply, lack of sufficient water, enemy raids on the fields—all probably caused or aggravated by the drought—must have led to internal strife and the development of factions. Families and entire villages began to abandon the northland. Mesa Verde

Keet Seel cliff dwelling in Navajo National Monument, Arizona.
(National Park Service)

and Utah people moved south and east, some into the Rio Grande area, some into the headwaters of the Zuni and Little Colorado rivers, and perhaps some into Hopi and Zuni country. Kayenta people also moved south, some into the Hopi country, and others farther on into the southern White Mountains.

Some archaeologists believe that the Pueblo people abandoned their homes because of nomadic invaders moving into the northern part of the Southwest from the north. Some of the descendants of the Desert Culture dwellers in Utah and Nevada, perhaps the ancestors of

45

the Ute and Paiute or other similar nomadic peoples, may have discovered that raids on the Pueblo fields of corn and storehouses were easier than hunting and gathering.

Yet there is little indication of warfare during this time. None of the large pueblos or cliff dwellings shows any signs of having been sacked and burned.

The Sinagua Indians around Flagstaff also cleared out of their homeland. As we saw in the last chapter, these Indians profited by the eruption of Sunset Crater in 1064–65. They adopted everything they could lay their hands on from the incoming wave of Hohokam, Mogollon, and Anasazi peoples. In fact, they adopted so much, particularly from the Anasazi, that you might have a hard time distinguishing between the two. Now they joined the southward migration, moving down the Verde River Valley, building towns such as Tuzigoot, sprawling down its hillside, and the cliff pueblo of Montezuma Castle. Then they, too, disappeared, and beyond this point we cannot, at present, trace them.

As the northern Pueblos moved southward, other populations were displaced. Many of the people south of the Little Colorado and along the upper Salt and Gila rivers began to press in upon the Hohokam. The Mimbres people moved out, perhaps into northern Mexico. By 1300 the whole northern frontier stood empty, or nearly so. The nomads and the few Pueblos who lingered there never again achieved the greatness of the Classic Period.

Archaeologists call the following period, that from 1300 to 1540, the Regressive Pueblo period. But this is probably a misnomer. It might better be termed the Golden Age, since despite withdrawals from outlying regions, the Anasazi built some of their largest pueblos at the time and produced some of their best pottery. The pueblos now tended to have central courts and the kivas became rectangular. Both the polychrome pottery and mural paintings in the kivas show a number of new life forms such as birds and mythological beasts and masked dancers, which some archaeologists attribute to influence from the Tlaloc religion of central Meso-America. They suggest, further, that this religion is the source of the Kachina Cult among the modern Pueblo Indians.

With this new period, new centers began to spring up. The Zuni country, Hopi mesas, Rio Grande Valley, mountainous areas of central Arizona and western New Mexico, and northern Mexico took the place of Chaco, Mesa Verde, and Kayenta. These areas offered permanent water, but each already maintained a sedentary population and the influx of new people meant overcrowding. Architecture and many of the arts degenerated. It was a period of disintegration before reintegration and renaissance.

Many towns of the period were very large, some covering ten to twelve acres. Usually these consisted of several rows of one- to three-storied houses built along streets or around open plazas. Kivas were again built in open courts. In the Hopi area and the central mountainous belt, kivas were rectangular with a bench or deep recess across one end. Ventilator, deflector, fire pit, and sipapu were present, as in earlier days. In contrast were the circular kivas of the Zuni, which seem a queer mixture of features from the small and great kivas of Chaco. In the mountainous belt the last great kivas were being made, but now they conformed to the rectangular style of smaller kivas and lacked some features of earlier ones.

Pottery also changed. Black-on-white, except for an occasional specimen, gave way to polychromes of black and white on red in a wide range of local and highly specialized types.

In the Rio Grande the earlier Pueblo peoples had just begun to establish themselves firmly when the great influx of northerners came. Soon large towns grew up. At Rito de Los Frijoles the circular, many-roomed pueblo of Tyuonyi was built at the base of towering cliffs of volcanic ash, in which other people dug caves to serve as back rooms to small pueblos built in front. Some towns, such as Pecos Pueblo a few miles east of the Rio Grande, had been built of stone masonry a century and a half before, but most houses were built of adobe or of stones in heavy adobe mortar.

Farther south along the Rio Grande, Mogollon people had lived in pithouses until about 1200, when the small adobe pueblo was introduced. These people were in contact with the Pueblo people of Chihuahua and through regular trade routes brought the produce of northern Mexico into Pueblo country.

Corrugated cooking ware died out, but painted wares were more elaborate. In the east they were characterized by lead glaze paint and in the west by an unglazed ware of highest artistic quality, known as Sikyatki polychrome. Sometime around 1300 a metallic glaze paint, evidently a local invention in east-central Arizona, was carried to the Rio Grande, where lead replaced copper as the key constituent.

Another idea that does not seem to occur widely and regularly in the Southwest before about 1300 is the formal arrangement of a town around a central plaza or several plazas, an inward-facing hollow-square type of layout. The source of, and reasons for, this change are unknown.

Further mass abandonments of large pueblos and en-

Prehistoric Pueblo black-on-white pottery.

(Tad Nichols)

tire districts occurred between 1450 and 1540. By 1500 only three centers remained: Hopi, Zuni-Acoma area, and the Rio Grande extending eastward to Pecos. Begun in the thirteenth century, Pecos continued as an important center until early in the nineteenth century. By 1450 the irrigated fields of the Hohokam seem to have been abandoned, and only smaller communities remained along the rivers and in the desert lands of southwestern Arizona.

In the western Arizona Desert and along the lower Colorado River, the Patayan, or Hakataya, had continued to exist with seemingly little change. Between 1450 and 1540 the wide expanse of country from Pinedale to Point of Pines had been relinquished, and the Sinagua had completely disappeared. The great houses of Chihuahua were abandoned. There seems to have been only comparatively rude settlers left in much of the Hohokam region of southern Arizona.

4

1540 and After

U P UNTIL the sixteenth century the Pueblo and Hohokam and other Southwestern Indians had the country
pretty much to themselves. If they fought or traded or
exchanged ideas, they fought or traded or exchanged
ideas with one another or with neighboring Indian tribes
to the north or south or east or west. Each camp or
village or town was more or less independent. Nobody
tried to force his way of life on anybody else.

But that idyllic situation couldn't last. In 1539 the
first invaders showed up. After Hernando Cortez conquered the Aztecs and other Mexican Indian tribes in
1520 and Francisco Pizarro liberated the Incas of Peru
a dozen years later, gold-hungry Spaniards began hunting for new lands to loot.

By the early 1530's, verbal accounts of the Pueblo
Indians and their multistoried apartment houses built of
stone and adobe, perhaps passed on from Indian trader
to Indian trader, had reached the ears of the Spaniards

in central Mexico. A few years later confirmation of these stories appeared in the person of Cabeza de Vaca and three equally half-naked, half-starved companions. These four were the survivors of an ill-fated Spanish expedition to Florida in 1528. Wrecked by a storm on the Texas coast, where most of their comrades were either drowned or eaten by cannibal Texans, De Vaca, a Negro or Moorish slave called Esteban, and two other Spaniards finally managed to escape from their Indian captors and headed westward. After eight years of almost incredible adventures and hardships, the castaways succeeded in reaching the Spanish settlements on the Pacific coast of Mexico.

During their wanderings they had heard tales of large and wealthy cities to the north, cities whose inhabitants had many cotton fabrics and turquoise ornaments. These stories so interested Antonio de Mendoza, then governor of New Spain, that he sent out a Franciscan monk, Fray Marcos de Niza, with Esteban as guide and interpreter, to investigate the rumors. Esteban and an escort of several hundred Mexican Indians went on ahead to scout out the trail. Esteban far outdistanced the friar and eventually reached the first of the pueblos, which archaeologists have identified as the Zuni Indian town of Hawikuh in west-central New Mexico on the border between Arizona and New Mexico. Just what happened there will never be known, as accounts differ. We do know that the Indians refused to let Esteban enter the pueblo and, after stripping him of his belongings, put him in a building outside the village. The next morning he was killed, along with some of his followers. The rest fled southward to carry the bad news to De Niza. Again accounts differ as to what happened next. Some say Fray Marcos immediately turned back for

Mexico and safety. Others, including Fray Marcos himself, said that he continued on until he could glimpse Hawikuh from a safe distance. Noting that it was even larger than Mexico City, he returned at once to Mexico.

De Niza's glowing, if slightly exaggerated, report was enough to set Mexico City on fire, like a nineteenth-century gold strike. Francisco Vásquez de Coronado and an army of Spanish soldiers and Mexican Indian attendants, together with Fray Marcos and several other friars, promptly headed north. Six months later, after a long hazardous march, the army reached Hawikuh on July 7, 1540. The Zunis bravely resisted the invaders. But the Indians found that bows and arrows and clubs were no match for gunpowder and armor and horses, and they were soon forced to surrender.

To put it mildly, Coronado and his followers were far from impressed with the half dozen Zuni towns and their inhabitants. Instead of discovering huge cities rich in gold and silver and precious jewels, all they could see were stone and adobe towns, all far smaller than Mexico City. To cap it all, there was no gold, no silver, and no precious stones except turquoise.

But Coronado didn't give up hope. Maybe there were other richer cities somewhere in this new land. Learning from the Zunis of more towns in a land called Tusayan off to the northwest, he sent Don Pedro de Tovar and a score of soldiers to investigate. They had no trouble finding the towns, seven of them built on top of four high mesas and occupied by Hopi Indians. (These Indians have also been popularly known as the Moqui, or Moki, Indians.) Caught by surprise at the easternmost pueblo of Awatovi, the Hopis sallied forth in battle array. After several natives were killed, however, the rest fled into the town and quickly sued for peace. Tovar soon found that the Hopis were little richer than the Zunis. The Hopis did tell him about a mighty river still farther to the west.

When Coronado was told about this, he sent Captain García López de Cárdenas and twenty-five horsemen to explore the area. After securing guides and provisions from the Hopis, Cárdenas went on west to discover the Grand Canyon of the Colorado River. But this national park's first tourists weren't too impressed with the mile-deep gorge. They were hunting for gold, not scenery.

Hearing of still more Indian towns to the east, Coronado sent out another party of soldiers, with Hernando de Alvarado in command. Alvarado discovered the pueblo of Acoma a short distance to the east, and went on to the Rio Grande where he found numerous other Indian pueblos up and down the river. Still farther to the east he visited the easternmost pueblo of Pecos, the largest Indian town he had seen.

Coronado and his army moved to the Rio Grande Valley to spend the winter in the Indian province called Tiguex, near the site of present-day Bernalillo, New Mexico. Upon request, the Indians moved out of one of the pueblos in order that the Spaniards might have warmer winter quarters.

At first the Indians were friendly and generous with their supplies. But trouble soon came. Trying to feed and clothe hundreds of Spanish soldiers and their Mexican Indian followers, plus hundreds of horses and unknown numbers of cattle and sheep, was no easy task. Frequently the Spaniards were overbearing and demanded a great deal more than could be provided on short notice. In addition, they imprisoned a number of Indian hostages and even put some to the third degree. The Pueblo Indians stood these and other injustices as

A section of the partially abandoned Hopi pueblo of Oraibi, the oldest continuously inhabited village in the United States.

(Tad Nichols)

long as they could. Finally, the Indians of the adjoining pueblo revolted against their uninvited guests, running off their herd of horses. The Spaniards laid siege to the pueblo and destroyed it, massacring several hundred of its inhabitants.

Coronado then demanded the submission of the rest of the pueblos in that province. But the Indians abandoned most of them and assembled for defense in two of the larger towns. Coronado immediately laid siege to them. The Indians managed to hold out for several months before they were defeated, many of them being killed and the rest captured as slaves.

From a captive Indian at Pecos, an imaginative Plains Indian whom the Spaniards named Turk, they learned of the land of Quivira, a marvelous land of gold and silver located out on the plains to the northeast. This was a lure the Spaniards couldn't resist. In the spring of 1541 Coronado and his army set out across the plains, with Turk and a second Plains Indian as guides. After months of exploring through Texas and Oklahoma, they finally reached the land of Quivira in what is now central Kansas. And once again the Spaniards were disappointed. The Indian villages they found were not even as rich as those of the Pueblo Indians in New Mexico. Moreover, now that Turk was back home, he began plotting to have the Spaniards killed. Coronado had had enough of the land of Quivira and its inhabitants. He had Turk executed for his treachery, and marched back to the Rio Grande.

After another cold, miserable winter there, he had also had enough of the Pueblo Indians and their land. In April, 1542, Coronado and his soldiers left for Mexico. Even though they had found no cities of gold and no fabulous treasures, most of them were glad to get out of the country with their lives. Two of the Franciscan friars did stay, one at the pueblo of Pecos and the other at Quivira. Both, however, were soon killed by the Indians.

The Pueblo Indians were equally happy to see the Spaniards go. They hoped they had seen the last of these bearded white men and their noisy, unearthly weapons and their huge, four-footed animals.

They had, at least for a time; Coronado's unfavorable reports discouraged further exploration for nearly forty years. Then, in 1581, Francisco Sanchez Chamuscado and a small party of soldiers escorted three Franciscans up the Rio Grande and left them there to try to convert the Pueblo Indians. A year later Antonio de Espejo and Friar Bernardino Beltran led an expedition north to find out what had happened to the three missionaries. They soon learned that all three had been killed by the Indians. Espejo then took the opportunity to do some exploring. Stopping at Acoma, Zuni, and the Hopi villages, he toured south through central Arizona and back to the Rio Grande and on to Pecos before returning to Mexico.

In 1590 still another Spanish expedition, this one led by Castano de Sosa, came up the Rio Grande. De Sosa intended to found a colony in the Pueblo country. However, he was soon overtaken by a second party that arrested him and his settlers for making unauthorized explorations.

Except for sowing the seeds of fear and resentment and distrust of the white man, these brief visits had little real effect on the Pueblo Indians. In between the expeditions the Indians went right on about their business as they had been doing for centuries.

In 1598, however, the Spaniards came back for good. Don Juan de Oñate was awarded a contract by the King of Spain for colonization of the Pueblo country. Oñate brought with him more than 100 soldiers, nearly 300 colonists, a number of Franciscan priests, 83 wagons, and 7,000 head of cattle, horses, and sheep. Marching up the Rio Grande from Chihuahua, Oñate established the first Spanish settlement in New Mexico at San Gabriel, just across the river from the Tewa Indian pueblo of San Juan. By the close of the century he had obtained the submission of the rest of the pueblos. Only with Acoma, the sky city, did he have any trouble, and this town on top of its high mesa was soon captured and many of its inhabitants were killed.

During the opening years of the seventeenth century, Oñate made a number of survey trips throughout the

The pueblo of Acoma, the Sky City, perched on top of a high mesa in western New Mexico.

(National Park Service)

Southwest. On one of these he explored up and down the Colorado River. The report of this trip shows that, then as now, you can't believe everything that you read. Father Escobar recorded everything they saw on this trip, fairly accurately as far as we can tell. But when he told what a native Indian chief said about some of the other people living along the Colorado, he left the field of fact for that of fiction. According to Escobar, the chief told him of a tribe of people whose ears were so long that they dragged on the ground, of another tribe of people with only one foot, of still another tribe that lived on smells, of a fourth tribe that slept underwater, of a fifth that slept standing up with burdens on their backs, and of a sixth that roosted in trees. More to the Spaniards' liking perhaps, he also told of a tribe using bowls made of silver and of a lake where the natives wore golden bracelets. Letting his imagination soar still more, he told of a nearby island where the men were bald.

In 1610, three years after the founding of Jamestown several thousand miles to the east, Oñate moved the capital of New Spain south to the town of Santa Fe, the site of a former Tewa Indian village. From this headquarters the Spaniards began the task of Christianizing and colonizing the Pueblo Indians.

One of their first jobs was the construction of mission buildings. These were huge, walled compounds located either within or just outside the Pueblo villages. They were built entirely by Indian labor under the supervision of the Franciscan friars. They were made of adobe or of sandstone slabs set in adobe mud. Since there weren't enough missionaries to go around, most of the missions were only what were called *visitas,* being visited by priests about once a month.

From their very first encounter, the Spaniards and the Pueblo Indians didn't get along too well. The civilian authorities, as well as the missionaries, abused the Indians by exacting tribute or labor or both from them. The Indians, as a conquered people, were treated as subjects, slaves, and servants. The soldiers, the settlers, and the missionaries all exploited the Indians, using the Indians in any way they could as free labor, yet at the same time expecting tribute in the form of corn or cloth or anything else they might need or want.

Although theoretically the missions were supposed to be training centers for the Indians, the Indians did all the work. Some were cooks and servants; some did leatherwork or weaving or blacksmithing. Others took care of the church gardens and orchards. Still others herded the mission's sheep and cattle. The Indians were forced to attend church services. At the same time the missionaries concentrated their efforts on stamping out Pueblo religious beliefs and practices. They raided the Pueblo ceremonial centers—the kivas—and burned their masks and prayer sticks. Some of the Pueblo religious leaders were whipped and hung as witches.

Almost all of the Spanish government officials spent a great deal of their time in various types of economic enterprises for their own profit. They set up workshops in which Indians wove cloth and blankets. Other Indians collected huge amounts of pinyon nuts, which could be sold for handsome profits in Mexico. Still other Indians built wagons and carts for trading caravans to Mexico and were even pressed into service as servants and muleteers on these same caravans. And all of the officials profited from the collection of tribute.

The soldiers and settlers, most of whom had their families with them, also profited from the Indians, using them as servants in their homes and as gardeners and herders to take care of their farms and livestock.

The Spaniards also imposed their own form of government on the Pueblo Indians, requiring each pueblo to appoint a set of officers. These were usually a governor, a lieutenant governor, a sheriff, a church assistant, ditch superintendents.

The Spanish contact did bring the Pueblo Indians numerous items of European civilization: horses, cattle, sheep, wheat, chili peppers, peaches, melons, and other new crops, along with true adobe bricks for building and metal tools.

But these didn't begin to offset the system of exploitation. The Pueblo Indians, by nature peaceful and not at all aggressive, were slow to react to the abuses and injustices to which they were continually subjected. But react they finally did. During the period from 1640 to 1680, there were half a dozen Pueblo revolts against their overlords. But these were all minor and local, and the Spaniards were easily able to suppress them.

Then came 1680. For the first and last time in their history, all of the Pueblo Indians united together in a common cause. Even the distant Hopi Indians in Arizona joined their eastern cousins. The uprising was led by a San Juan Tewa Indian named Pope. Pope had been one of nearly fifty Indian religious leaders given a public whipping in Santa Fe in 1675. To get revenge, he planned a general revolt against the Spaniards. But there were too many in on the plot. The news leaked out, and the Indians had to strike ahead of time. Unfortunately for the Spaniards, most of them paid little attention to the warning. They had heard similar warnings many times before. When they finally discovered that this time it was the real thing, it was too late. After a bloody three weeks of fighting, bows and arrows won out over gunpowder and horses. Although 2,000 Spanish settlers fled south to the safety of what is now El Paso, Texas, 21 missionaries and nearly 400 Spanish soldiers and colonists lost their lives. So did hundreds of Indians.

The Pueblo Indians celebrated their victory, which we might call the first American Revolution, by destroying the churches and missions, burning their furnishings and records, and wiping out all other signs of the hated Spaniards.

But they celebrated too soon. Each of the pueblos was used to being independent. Once the fighting was over and the Spaniards had left, the pueblos went right back to being individual towns again. Consequently, in 1692–

93, when Diego de Vargas, along with a well-equipped army, showed up, he was able to reestablish control in Santa Fe without firing a shot. Most of the other pueblos also submitted without a struggle. Some Indians took to the hills, raiding and harassing the Spanish settlements. Eventually, they, too, were forced to sue for peace and were returned to their villages.

The Spaniards wasted no time in clamping their heavy-handed rule over the Indians, taking their land and using the Indians as servants and slaves, reconverting the Indians and rebuilding the churches.

After several brief flare-ups of resentment, during the summer of 1696 Indians from half a dozen pueblos again rose up in rebellion against Spanish authority, killing six priests and a score of other Spaniards. De Vargas captured some of the leaders, but large numbers of Indians fled to the Navaho and Hopi country. By the early 1700's some of these peoples had returned to their homeland. But others stayed away for half a century.

But there was one Pueblo region the Spaniards never did reconquer. That was the Hopi country. Like the Rio Grande Pueblos, the Hopis had joined the rebellion of 1680 and had killed all their resident missionaries and destroyed the missions and their furnishings. In 1692 the Hopis did submit to De Vargas and his superior military force. But only Awatovi, the easternmost of the Hopi villages, allowed Spanish missionaries to return and rebuild their church. The other Hopis, along with the Rio Grande refugees living with them, didn't like this. In fact, so strong was their feeling that they decided to destroy Awatovi. In 1700, under the leadership of the Oraibi chief, warriors from all of the other Hopi villages sacked Awatovi, killing almost the entire population of some eight hundred. The town of Awatovi was completely destroyed and was never again rebuilt or re-occupied. Several times the Spaniards sent military expeditions against the Hopis. But each time the Hopis and their Rio Grande refugee neighbors turned them back.

At about this same time these Rio Grande refugees decided to stay in the Hopi country, where they would be far away from the Spaniards. They built their own town of Hano right next to one of the Hopi towns. There they still live today, still speaking their own distinct language.

After the final reconquest, the Pueblo Indians of New Mexico never again challenged Spanish rule. While outwardly accepting Spanish authority and the Catholic religion, they carried on a passive resistance.

Arizona and the rest of the western part of the Southwest was largely bypassed by the Spaniards until the late 1600's. Then Spanish missionaries came up the Santa Cruz and San Pedro river valleys about as far north as the present-day town of Tucson, establishing missions among the Papago Indians. But that was just about as far north as they got. The Chiricahua and Western Apache Indians saw to it that these white-skinned invaders pushed no farther north.

5

The People and Their Languages

ACCORDING to archaeologists, there were about 103,000 Indians living in the Southwest when the first Europeans arrived in 1539–40.

There were twenty or thirty different Indian tribes living there then: the Hopi, Zuni, and Rio Grande Pueblo Indians in northern Arizona and New Mexico, the Pima and Papago in Southern Arizona, the Yuma, Cocopa, Maricopa, Chemehuevi, Mohave, Havasupai, Walapai, and Yavapai along the Colorado River in the west and northwest, the Ute and Paiute on the northern fringes of the area, and the Navaho, Western Apache, Chiricahua Apache, Mescalero Apache, and Jicarilla Apache on the north and east.

Most, if not all, of the archaeological ancestors of these tribes can be identified. In northern Arizona and New Mexico the present Pueblo Indians still live in the towns or on the sites of their ancestors, the Anasazi. The Hopis are the lineal descendants of the prehistoric

Pueblo Indians who used to live in northeastern Arizona, while the Rio Grande Pueblo Indians can trace their ancestry back to the cliff dwellers and pueblo peoples of Mesa Verde and northwestern New Mexico. The Zuni and Acoma peoples, however, probably represent a merging of Mogollon and Anasazi and perhaps other prehistoric groups in eastern Arizona and western New Mexico.

Along the Colorado River, the historic Yuma, Mohave, Yavapai, Havasupai, and Walapai Indians are believed to be the descendants of the prehistoric Patayan peoples. They were, at any rate, living in the territory formerly occupied by Patayan peoples when the first Spaniards arrived.

In the southern and central Arizona deserts, the present-day Pima and Papago Indians are the probable descendants of the ancient Hohokam peoples. This has, however, not as yet been proved to the satisfaction of all anthropologists.

These diverse backgrounds also show up in language. All languages spoken by members of Southwestern Indian tribes differ radically from English. Furthermore, they frequently vary as much or more from one another. Contrary to popular opinion, all Indians don't speak the same language. There are nearly as many different languages and dialects among the Southwestern Indians as there are tribes.

Language experts, called linguists, classify languages by grouping them into families. That is, languages that show relationships to one another, through their structure and grammar and vocabularies, must therefore have had a common ancestry. Thus our English, along with German and French and Greek and Russian, belongs to the Indo-European language family. In the

The chief Antelope priest of the Hopi pueblo of Walpi.
*(Smithsonian Office of Anthropology,
Bureau of American Ethnology Collection)*

same way linguists tell us that the languages of the Southwestern Indians belong to half a dozen different language families: Athabascan, Uto-Aztecan, Tanoan, Keresan, Yuman, and Zunian.

Let's take the Pueblo Indians as an example. You might think that the Pueblo Indians, sharing a common culture and living relatively close together, would all speak the same language. But they do not. There are at least four distinct languages: Hopi, Zuni, Tanoan, and Keresan.

All of the Hopi Indians speak the same language, a Shoshonean language belonging to the Uto-Aztecan family. The Zuni Indians also speak the same language, Zuni, which seems to be a separate language group, with no close relatives. This also applies to Keresan, or Keres, the language spoken at seven of the New Mexico pueblos: Cochiti, Santo Domingo, San Felipe, Santa Ana, Zia (or Sia), Laguna, and Acoma. There are only minor differences between the Acoma dialect and that spoken at the Rio Grande pueblos.

The rest of the New Mexico Pueblo Indians speak one or another of three related languages belonging to the Tanoan family—Tiwa, Tewa, and Towa. The people of the pueblos of Isleta, Sandia, Picuris, and Taos speak dialects of the Tiwa language. But some of these Tiwa-speaking Indians have trouble understanding their neighbors. The people of Isleta and Sandia don't have any trouble talking to one another. Nor do the Indians of Picuris and Taos. Yet, while the people of Isleta and Sandia can understand the dialects spoken at Picuris and Taos, the Indians of Picuris and Taos have a difficult time understanding their southern relatives. Tiwa was formerly spoken by Indians who lived in now-abandoned villages in the area south of Santa Fe and also among the extinct Piro and other pueblos still farther south along the Rio Grande. The Indians at San Juan, San Ildefonso, Santa Clara, Nambe, Pojoaque, and Tesuque speak the Tewa language. Tewa is also spoken at Hano, the Tanoan village built on First Mesa in the Hopi country by a group of Indians who migrated from the Rio Grande after the Pueblo Rebellion of 1680. The only Indians speaking the third Tanoan language, Towa, are those living in the pueblo of Jemez, including the descendants of the Indians who abandoned Pecos Pueblo in 1838.

According to many linguists, Tanoan is remotely related to the Uto-Aztecan family and should be included, along with Hopi, in a larger family called the Aztec-Tanoan language family.

Down in southern Arizona the Pima and Papago languages are related to Shoshonean (Hopi) and thus also can be pigeonholed in the Aztec-Tanoan family. Pima and Papago Indians actually speak almost the same language, the two dialects differing from each other no more than varieties in our American English. The Yaqui (many of whom live in and around Tucson and Phoenix as refugees from Mexico) language is related to Pima and Papago. But it is not close enough so that they can understand one another. Other northern Mexican Indian tribes, such as the Opata, Tarahumare, and Cahita, also belong to the Aztec-Tanoan language family.

Still other Southwestern peoples speaking languages of the Aztec-Tanoan family are the Shoshonean-speaking Indians in Colorado, Utah, southern Nevada, and eastern California. These Indians—the Ute, southern Paiute, and Chemehuevi—speak languages that are distantly related to Hopi. The languages of the Chemehuevi and Southern Paiute are similar enough to allow members of the two tribes to talk to one another.

We might even bring in yet another Shoshonean-speaking people, the Comanche, and call them Southwestern. Actually, the Comanche were one of the numerous Plains Indian tribes, famous as raiders and fighters. After separating from their brothers, the Shoshone, somewhere up in Wyoming perhaps, they moved southward through the high plains. By 1700 they were located along the Texas-New Mexico border and repeatedly raided and traded with the New Mexico Pueblo Indians.

In western Arizona and the eastern fringe of California, along the Colorado River Valley, seven Indian tribes use dialects of the Yuman language. These are the Yumas, Cocopas, Mohaves, Maricopas, Walapais, Ya-

Navaho Indian family.

(Tad Nichols)

vapais, and Havasupais. In spite of a great many similarities, however, not all of these people can speak with or understand members of the other tribes. Cocopas, for example, cannot talk with or understand any of the others. Mohaves and Maricopas speak similar dialects, as do Walapais, Havasupais, and Yavapais.

The last of our language families in the Southwest is the Athabascan. This is the family to which some of our most noted Indian tribes belong—the Navaho and Apache. These Athabascan-speaking Indians are relative newcomers to the region. Their nearest linguistic relatives are located several thousand miles to the north in Canada and Alaska, with a few others scattered along the Pacific coast from British Columbia south to northern California. For some unknown reason one or more groups of these northern hunters broke off from the others and began to push their way southward. How and when they came we don't know.

Many anthropologists say they drifted down the eastern foothills of the Rocky Mountains, reaching the Southwest perhaps by the early sixteenth century, not too many years before the first Spaniards came up from the south. Some archaeologists, however, think that the Apaches may have reached the Southwest as early as the thirteenth century and may, therefore, have been at least partially responsible for raiding the Pueblo Indians and forcing them to abandon their northern cliff dwellings and pueblos.

We don't know when or why these intruders from the north split up. But split up they did into seven distinct groups, or tribes—Navaho, Western Apache, Chiricahua Apache, Mescalero Apache, Jicarilla Apache, Lipan Apache, and Kiowa Apache. By the middle of the nineteenth century the Jicarilla ranged over northeastern

Western Apache man at Whiteriver, Arizona.
(Tad Nichols)

New Mexico and southeastern Colorado; the Mescalero in south-central New Mexico east of the Rio Grande; the Chiricahua in southeastern Arizona, southwestern New Mexico, and northern Mexico; the Western Apache in eastern Arizona; and the Navaho in northwestern New Mexico and northeastern Arizona. The last two Apache groups lived out on the plains: the Kiowa Apache in southeastern Kansas, western Oklahoma, and the northern part of the the Texas Panhandle; and the Lipan farther to the south in Texas and northern Mexico.

All of these Apache tribes, including the Navaho, speak languages which are closely related to one another.

Although some people claim that "If you've seen one Indian, you've seen them all," not all Indians look alike. There is no more a typical Southwestern Indian than there is a typical twentieth-century Southwestern American. The Southwest was just as much a melting pot in A.D. 1 as it is today.

Most Indians do, however, have a great many physical characteristics in common—brown or reddish-brown skin, straight and usually coarse black hair, little beard or body hair, dark-brown to black eyes, and generally broad and high cheekbones. These things cause physical anthropologists (those scientists who study man's bones and other physical features) to class the American Indian as a member of the Mongoloid race.

But Indians vary from tribe to tribe. Some are short, some tall; some are stocky, some skinny; some have long and narrow skulls, some broad or almost round heads; some have straight noses, some hawklike noses; some are rather narrow-faced, some broader-faced.

In the Southwest, for example, the Mohaves and Pimas and Maricopas are fairly tall, many men measur-
72

ing 6 feet. The Zuni and Hopi and a majority of the other Pueblo Indians are short and stocky, the men averaging about 5 feet 4 or 5 inches in stature. In general, the Navaho and most other Apache groups are taller than the Pueblos but shorter than the Mohaves and Pimas and Yumans.

6

The Pueblo Cornplanters

Of THE 103,000 Indians living in the Southwest when the first Spaniards arrived in 1539–40, 30,000 were Pueblos.

All of these Pueblo Indians live today in approximately the same locations as they did at the time of the Spanish Conquest. At that time there were around 75 or 80 inhabited pueblos. Today, four hundred years later, there are only some 30 villages left. The Pueblo Indians have, however, increased in numbers, particularly since 1900, when there were only about 10,000 of them left. The latest population figures show them rapidly approaching the 30,000 mark.

Yet even after four hundred years of rule by Spaniards and Mexicans and Americans, the life of the Pueblos of today is surprisingly like that of their ancestors of the sixteenth and seventeenth centuries.

Architecture and the building of houses, farming and farming practices, religious and ceremonial affairs, and

Pueblo of Zuni in 1879.
(Smithsonian Office of Anthropology,
Bureau of American Ethnology Collection)

the social system of the Pueblo Indians have been affected relatively little by their nearly four centuries of association with the whites. But many of their native arts, with the exception of pottery making, have practically disappeared, particularly since the American occupation during the middle of the nineteenth century and its influx of good tools and new textile fabrics.

The most characteristic feature of Pueblo Indian life is the pueblo itself, the odd type of village that has given the culture its name. A pueblo, as we have seen, is a compact collection of rectangular, flat-roofed rooms, built up against one another to form a compact village unit, like a giant apartment house, which houses an entire community.

The general plan of the pueblo has remained essentially unchanged since prehistoric times. The rooms may be grouped in a single solid mass or, more commonly today, in two or more clusters of buildings, sometimes irregularly arranged in long rows about an open courtyard or two. These village units were usually from two to four or five stories high and were terraced, rooms rising one behind the other like giant stairs. The roof of one story served as the floor of the one directly above.

Today Zuni and Taos are the only real Pueblo skyscrapers, reaching a height of five stories. At the pueblos of Santa Clara and Jemez the buildings are built on the four sides of a court, each apartment house terraced back from the court.

In aboriginal times the lower story rooms in the outer tier had no doorways or openings of any kind. They were entered by means of notched log ladders through square openings or hatchways in the roof. To get inside the pueblo, you had to climb a similar pole ladder from the ground up to the roof of the first balcony, from that to the second balcony, and so on.

Upper floor rooms usually had external doorways opening out onto the balcony or leading back into interior rooms. These doorways, however, were generally so low and narrow that they were difficult to squeeze through. Some were built at floor level. But most were from 1 to 3 feet above the floor. The doorways themselves were about 2 feet wide and 3 to 4 feet high.

The western Pueblos, like Acoma, Zuni, and Hopi, were built largely of flat slabs of sandstone, the comparatively soft, red or yellow rock so abundant throughout the mesa country of northern Arizona. The Rio Grande Pueblos, however, had little stone available and were forced to use adobe. This natural mixture of clay and sand is abundant all over Arizona and New Mexico. When mixed with water, it dries as hard as stucco. Coated thickly over poles and brush, it made a solid wall. Or mixed with river stones and placed in handfuls on a wall, it dried like the clay in pottery. In fact, since the western Indians invariably plastered over their stone walls, both inside and out, with adobe mud, the houses in the two regions looked a lot alike.

Each family lived in one or two of the rooms in the upper and outer tier of rooms, where there was light and where the people could use the balconies or terraces as cooking and work areas. This left the darker inner rooms on the lower floors for use as storerooms or, occasionally, as living rooms during the colder winter months.

Home furnishings were few—a stone- or clay-lined fire pit in the center of the room, a built-in bench of clay-plastered logs or stones along one wall, small wall niches serving as cupboards, sometimes a pole clothes rack suspended from the log rafters by yucca fiber string, and often a mealing or grinding bin on one side of the room where corn could be ground on two or three metates, perhaps the most important piece of furniture of all.

In former days the smoke from the fire pit found its way out through the hatchway in the roof or through the doorway, if the room had one, or through cracks in the wall. After the Spaniards came the fireplace was moved to the corner of the room, with a flue to catch the smoke and take it out through a chimney on top of the roof. The oldest form of chimney consisted of several circular

Kiva in San Ildefonso pueblo, New Mexico.
(Arizona State Museum)

courses of stone laid in adobe mud and topped with a
discarded cooking pot, the bottom of which had been
knocked out. Sometimes two or three such jars were
placed one above the other to form a higher chimney.
Now, of course, stone and adobe flue construction is
more common, although sheet metal stovepipe is also
being used more and more.

Today there are other Spanish and later American influences, including stairways, windows and glass windowpanes and full-sized doorways equipped with wooden doors. Whenever new houses are built or added on to the older ones, they are usually only one story.

A picturesque feature of most pueblos today is the beehive- or dome-shaped outside oven made of clay and stone and smoothly plastered. In spite of its ancient look, however, this style of oven is not Indian. It was borrowed from the Spanish during early historic times.

The average pueblo probably accommodated about two or three hundred people. Some, of course, were considerably larger. Hawikuh, for example, seems to have had a population of around six hundred. It was the largest of the six Zuni pueblos, consisting of six groups of solidly massed stone rooms, each from one to three stories high. There were, according to archaeologists, about one thousand rooms in Hawikuh, but probably not more than four or five hundred were lived in or used at any one time. Founded as far back as the thirteenth century, Hawikuh was occupied for some four hundred years. After the Pueblo Rebellion of 1680, Hawikuh, along with the five other Zuni towns, was abandoned and the entire tribe built and moved into the present pueblo of Zuni.

Along with its living rooms and storerooms, each pueblo had its secret ceremonial chambers, its kivas. In the Rio Grande pueblos, with the exception of Jemez, the kivas are circular, semisubterranean rooms like those of their ancestors, the Anasazi. At Jemez, Acoma, and Zuni the ceremonial rooms are rectangular, aboveground structures built into the house block. Hopi kivas, on the other hand, are not only rectangular but also semisubterranean. In these kivas are held the secret ceremonial rites of various religious organizations. Kivas are also important as council chambers.

The kiva has its social side as well. It serves as a workshop for those who want to weave or make arrows or do other work. And it also serves as a clubroom or lounging place for those who just want to sit around and talk. In fact, many of the men may even sleep there when they want to escape from the women of their household for a night or two.

Except for ceremonial costumes, old-time Pueblo dress styles have all but disappeared. In prehistoric days the Pueblo Indians were the only Indians north of Mexico who wore clothing made of cotton cloth. Some skins were, of course, used for clothing, but cotton seems to have predominated. Men formerly wore a cotton loincloth, with another piece of the same material wrapped around the waist to form a kilt about a foot and a half long. Some women still wear the traditional dress consisting of a rectangular piece of cotton cloth fastened over the right shoulder and under the left arm, leaving the left shoulder bare. A long woven belt or sash, wrapped several times around the waist, holds the dress together. Today, however, these dresses are commonly made of wool. Both men and women formerly wore yucca sandals like those of their Anasazi ancestors. But in Spanish days they adopted deerskin moccasins with hard rawhide soles. During colder weather, in aboriginal times, men and women wore blankets of twisted strips of rabbit fur. Now most of them wear Navaho Indian blankets or commercial blankets.

The Pueblo Indians were and still are primarily farmers. Their main crop was and is Indian corn. But, although we think of corn as being either yellow or white, Pueblo corn was of many colors—blue, yellow, red or pink, white, black or dark purple, and speckled. A bunch of ears of corn hanging from a roof beam had as many different shades as a bouquet of wild flowers. Several varieties of beans and squash were also planted. Like corn, beans often came in many shades of red and white, or they were spotted. The Hopi Indians also planted sunflowers and raised them for their seeds, which are a good source of oil.

These are the old-time crops. Today, since Spanish days, most Pueblo Indians also raise wheat and alfalfa, along with such garden plants as onions, chili peppers, lettuce, peas, beets, tomatoes, and watermelons. Many of them have peach and apricot orchards, even the Hopi in their almost waterless desert country.

The Pueblo Indians are expert farmers. They can and do grow crops in places and under conditions that appear to be absolutely impossible. The western Pueblo Indians, the Hopi and Zuni, were dry farmers, locating their fields at the mouths of washes where they could take advantage of the runoff from summer rains. The three chief reasons for their success are deep planting, careful cultivation and weeding, and, above all, the right choice of ground.

Unlike the Hopi and Zuni country, the Rio Grande region provides a permanent water supply. There the Indians farmed the river bottoms where they could irrigate their fields by means of ditches. Where farming among the Hopi and Zuni was more of an individual or a family effort, among the Rio Grande Pueblos the tasks of clearing, terracing, damming, and ditching required greater community effort.

The wooden digging stick seems to have been the only aid to planting and cultivation. Even today not all Pueblo Indians own plows. Many of them still prefer the simple but efficient old-time digging sticks and hoes.

Men and women worked together in the building and

Hopi woman in dress of 1893.
(Smithsonian Office of Anthropology,
Bureau of American Ethnology Collection)

cleaning of the irrigation ditches and in the harvest. Men planted and tilled the fields and gardens and cut and brought in the firewood. Men also hunted, dressed the skins of the animals they killed, made their own bows and arrows and shields and war clubs, and wove blankets and sashes. Women took care of the children, did the cooking, ground the meal, and made the pottery. While men did the heavy work of hauling stone and roof timbers for the construction of houses, women did the plastering.

Although hunting and gathering are of little significance today, they were highly important in the past, particularly during years of crop failure. Cultivated crops were fresh only once a year, at harvest time. During the rest of the year the people had to eat corn, beans, and squash in dried form. To vary their diet with fresh vegetables, they had to hunt for wild roots and berries and greens. The women gathered all kinds of wild seeds, roots, fruits, and nuts—milkweed, pigweed, clover, sunflowers, rabbit brush, dandelions, cattails, saltbush, yucca, mustard plants, wild plums, walnuts, pinyon nuts, acorns, and a dozen different varieties of cactus, to name only a few.

Hunting was equally important in early days. Not only did the people need meat to supplement their otherwise strictly vegetarian diet, but they also needed skins for clothing, sinew for bowstrings and all types of fastenings, bone for awls and punches and other tools, and hooves for rattles. Most Pueblo Indians hunted rabbits, gophers, ground squirrels, deer, antelope, and mountain sheep. Those who lived near the Plains, like the Indians of Taos and Pecos, hunted buffalo, trading the robes to the Indians who lived farther to the west. They also caught a great many birds, particularly eagles and hawks, not for food but for their feathers for use in ceremonies.

Rabbits were abundant and were usually hunted by large groups of men and boys who surrounded a wide area and gradually moved inward, drawing the circle tighter and tighter. The entrapped rabbits were then killed with bows and arrows or with curved wooden throwing sticks shaped like boomerangs, although these wouldn't return to the thrower. Even today rabbits are still sometimes hunted in the old communal drives, probably more for the fun of it than for any actual need for rabbit meat.

Like a great many other Southwestern Indians, the Pueblos had a horror of anything living in the water and tabooed the eating of fish. This didn't lose them too much food since there were few rivers in the Southwest that had fish.

The only domestic animals these Indians had was the dog, which was not eaten, and the turkey, raised for its feathers rather than for its meat. Today Hopis and Zunis and other Pueblo Indians raise sheep, selling or weaving the wool and eating the meat.

Indian corn was the main food of the Pueblo Indians. Most of them thought corn to be sacred, a gift of the gods. There was hardly a ceremony in which corn or cornmeal was not used. Corn is still ground into meal on stone metates, and forms the chief ingredient in many dishes. Paper-thin cornmeal bread, like the many-colored *piki* bread of the Hopis, is a staple food item and is cooked on a stone griddle.

The social, political, and religious organizations of the Pueblo Indians are highly complex. They are so tightly interwoven that it is hard to determine where one leaves off and the other begins.

The Pueblo Indians do not form a tribe. Although there are many more similarities than differences among the pueblos, each major village is an independent unit in itself. In general, each pueblo is a strongly self-contained, closely knit unit, independent of all other pueblos. Essentially democratic as far as wealth and living conditions are concerned, it is governed by elective officers who handle both civil and religious affairs. The people visit back and forth, trading with each other. Yet at the same time they hold themselves apart. And while marriage outside one's own pueblo is not expressly forbidden, it is not favored either and is often made as difficult as possible.

The peace-loving Pueblos heavily emphasize community solidarity. Throughout the region individual behavior and achievement are subordinated to group activity.

The division between the eastern and western pueblos is most marked in social and ceremonial life. The household is the basic unit around which all social and religious organization revolves. The most important unit of social organization among the western pueblos is the clan, the group of blood relatives which traces descent in the female line, through the mother. Here women own the house, the furnishings, and the stores of food. At marriage a man takes up his residence at the house of his wife's parents. The women of the household own the fields.

The basic economic and social unit at Zuni, as well as at Hopi, and the one which is the most important in the business of daily living, is the household. This is an extended family, of which the maternal line is the core. Because everyone in a community shared one or more large apartment houses with everyone else in the pueblo, separate housing for extended families wasn't possible.

However, the members of a matrilocal extended family occupied adjoining, and often connecting, rooms or a series of such rooms.

Residence is matrilocal, as anthropologists call it, which simply means that the husband must move in with his wife and his wife's family. In such a matrilineal social structure, descent is traced through the female line, not the male. Property and the right to ceremonial and political office are also passed on through the female line. The ritual activities of the household and the clan are taken care of by the brothers and mother's brothers of the women, not by the husbands. The husbands who marry into the family and household and clan are looked on more or less as outsiders. They have few rights and, beyond furnishing economic support, play a more or less passive role, not interfering in household and clan affairs. A man's real home is his mother's house. There he keeps his important ritual paraphernalia, there he advises and disciplines his sister's children, and there he returns in case he and his wife split up.

Like many other Indians, the Pueblos look on marriage as the only true way for people to live. A bachelor or spinster is rare in Pueblo society. Marriage among the Pueblo Indians is strictly monogamous, just as it is with us.

The other western Pueblos, Zuni and Acoma, differ somewhat from the Hopi social pattern. Zuni, for example, represents a combination or consolidation of some six villages into one closely knit tribal group. Clan organization is not quite as strong in Zuni as it is among the Hopi. There are only thirteen matrilineal, exogamous, named clans, and these are probably of less importance in the Zuni social structure than is the household. Zuni clans have no political functions and lack both a clan head and a clan council.

In direct contrast to the western Pueblos, clans are unimportant or lacking among the eastern Pueblos along the Rio Grande. The Tiwa and Tewa pueblos, for example, are strongly patrilinear and patrilocal. Men generally own the houses and also generally inherit all of the property. There are no clans, and the chief social unit is the extended family.

Most of the eastern Pueblos are divided into two cere-monial moieties (from a French word meaning one-half), with all of the people of the village belonging to one moiety or the other. In contrast to the matrilineal Hopi and Zuni clans, these dual divisions are patrilineal, children being initiated into the moiety to which their father belongs. Moieties are primarily religious, not social units. They are associated with the summer and winter seasons and are known as the Summer People and the Winter People or as the Squash People and the Turquoise People. Each moiety is responsible for the governmental and ceremonial activities of the pueblo during its half of the year. Each is headed by a chief priest or *cacique* (a term of West Indian origin which was introduced by the Spanish), who is assisted by sev-eral society chiefs and other officials. The summer and winter *caciques* and their assistants organize the pueb-lo's ceremonies and dances, the cleaning and purifica-tion of the village, the construction and cleaning of the irrigation ditches, the repair of kivas and other com-munal property, and all planting and harvesting activ-ities. If any members of the village do not obey the offi-cials, they are subject to the penalty of fines or other punishment, including expulsion from the pueblo and confiscation of property.

While the Pueblo Indians were a lot less warlike than most of their neighbors, they could not have survived long without some military activity. All of the towns had a war priest who, in most cases, led the fighting force on raids. This warrior society served equally as a police force within the pueblo and a military force on the outside. Like most peaceful peoples, however, they usually waited until they were attacked before they began to fight back.

Perhaps the most striking feature of Pueblo culture is its native religion, which penetrates every aspect of Pueblo life. It is impossible to understand Pueblo life without knowing about native Pueblo religion. There is an almost endless parade of ceremonies and rituals throughout the year. Anthropologists estimate that Pueblo men spend at least half their time in religious activities. Few weeks are without their ceremonies.

Summer ceremonies generally deal with the bringing of rain and keeping the crops growing and prayers for abundant harvests, whereas the winter rites concentrate on fertility, medicine or curing, and war.

Most ceremonies are performed by dance societies or kiva groups, each headed by one or more priests. Each of these secret ceremonial organizations supervises some particular religious activity—war, healing, farming, hunting, rain (water spirits), magic, or kachinas. Each has its own set of rites and ceremonies and its own set of songs and dances, as well as its own altars and prayer sticks and costumes and other ceremonial paraphernalia. Many of these ceremonies are elaborate dramas, a blend of songs, dances, the rhythm of rattles and flutes and drums, mythology, imitative magic, and symbolism.

Most ceremonies begin with secret preliminary rites in the kiva or ceremonial chamber, where the society members, under the direction of the priests, fast, purify themselves, prepare altars and fetishes, and make offerings of feathered prayer sticks. These are believed to carry their prayers to the gods. The secret rites, which may last for eight or nine days, are usually followed by a public performance in the town plaza, where groups of dancers frequently masked and almost invariably symbolically painted and costumed, act out the final stages of the ceremony. Ritual smoking was an important feature of many ceremonies, often beginning and ending them.

The principal Pueblo gods or deities are the sun and the earth mother, along with wind, cloud, and thunder spirits and other supernatural beings. Among the Hopi and Zuni Indians particularly, ceremonies center on the kachinas, the spirits of departed ancestors. Through their association with clouds and rain, these supernatural beings control the weather. During certain ceremonies the kachinas are impersonated by men wearing masks and elaborate costumes. The Hopi ceremonial calendar sets aside half the year, from December to July, for masked kachina dances. The Hopis recognize over two hundred different kachinas. Some of these are female kachinas, which are always impersonated by men. Many kachinas are named for birds and animals—Hummingbird, Eagle, Bear, and Badger kachinas—while others have such descriptive names as Left-handed Kachina, Cross-legged Kachina, and Long-haired Kachina.

Each pueblo or group of villages speaking the same language has its own special ceremonies and ceremonial societies. Among the Rio Grande pueblos two of the most prominent societies are the Koshari and Kurena (both Keresan names). Both have to do with fertility and the growth of crops, the Koshari and Kurena serving as mediators between the Pueblo people and their ancient spirits. Members of both societies often act as clowns, as do some kachinas, to afford comic relief in the midst of other, more serious dances. Other Rio Grande dances are the Corn, Eagle, Buffalo, Basket, Bow and Arrow, Feather, Hoop, Sun, Butterfly, Turtle, and War and Peace dances. Some of the eastern Pueblos have even borrowed Comanche and Kiowa dances from the Plains Indians. Most of the Rio Grande Pueblos also have curing or healing societies, each usually concerning itself with certain particular ailments.

One of the most impressive of the Zuni ceremonies is the Shalako. This is a kachina or masked dance opening the new year for the Zunis. The Shalakos, wearing enormous wooden masks, bless the village and light new fires for the coming year.

Although the Hopi Snake Dance is neither the most elaborate nor the most important on the Hopi ceremonial calendar, it is by far the most spectacular and the most famous. Held annually in late August, this is a nine-day rain-making ceremony put on by members of the Snake and Antelope societies. During the first eight days the Snake and Antelope priests hold secret prayers and rituals in their respective kivas. On four of those days the Snake priests scour the desert for snakes in each of the four directions. Rattlesnakes are preferred, but red racers and bull snakes are also collected if not enough rattlesnakes turn up. On the afternoon of the ninth day the Snake and Antelope priests put on their war paint and array themselves in their best ceremonial kilts and ornaments and rattles. Moving to the village plaza, the Antelope priests dance and sing and shake gourd rattles. At the same time the Snake priests dance around the plaza in trios, one holding a snake in his mouth while the second strokes it with an eagle-feather whip. After circling the plaza four times, the dancer drops the snake, which is picked up by the gatherer, the third member of

90

Hopi Indian Snake Dance at Mishongnovi pueblo in 1885.
*(Smithsonian Office of Anthropology,
Bureau of American Ethnology Collection)*

the trio. After all of the snakes have been carried around
the plaza, they are placed in a charmed circle and
sprinkled with sacred cornmeal. Then each priest grabs
as many wriggling snakes as he can hold and runs to the
bottom of the mesa where he sets them free in one or the
other of the four directions. The snakes, being thought
of as messengers of the gods, carry the songs and prayers
of the Hopi to the gods. And during the next few days,
rain seldom fails to fall in answer to these rites and

prayers. (I know from personal experience, as I have been caught in sudden desert rainstorms on the two occasions that I have witnessed Hopi Snake Dances.)

Don't ask me why these Snake priests rarely get bitten by the rattlesnakes they carry around in their mouths and hands. The Hopis do not remove the fangs, nor do they dope the snakes. Careful handling and herding with other snakes may furnish a partial explanation. And stroking the snakes with feather whips certainly helps to keep them calm. The Snake priests themselves believe that they are immune during the ceremony because of their brotherly relationship, as members of the Snake Society, to the snakes. Psychologically, this undoubtedly also helps.

The Hopis also have a Kachina Bean Planting Ceremony, a Niman Kachina Ceremony celebrating the departure of the kachinas in July, a nine-day Flute Ceremony in August, a New Fire Ceremony, and Basket, Harvest, Butterfly, and Buffalo dances.

Nearly every Pueblo ceremony, whether it is only a one-day dance or a nine-day ceremony, is also a social occasion for the village. Friends and relatives come from the neighboring towns to see the dances, to help eat the food that is always prepared for the accompanying feasts, to gossip, and to play games. Most Pueblo religious ceremonies have their ceremonial foot races or kicking races, in which a block of wood or a stone ball is kicked around a course laid out across the desert.

7

The Desert Dwellers of the Southwest

THE SOUTHERN and western Arizona desert country is a hot and dry land of sand and cactus and lizards and rattlesnakes. It is also the home of the Pima and Papago and half a dozen other Indian tribes, tribes that have discovered how to make a living from their harsh environment.

These desert tribes include three geographic groups, groups that are alike in their ability to wrest a living from the desert but that differ widely in language and customs.

The first group, living in south-central and southwestern Arizona, includes the Pima and Papago Indians, closely related in language, and the Maricopa, who speak a totally different tongue. The Maricopa, a Yuma-speaking tribe that once lived near the junction of the Gila and Colorado rivers, were forced from their former home by the Yuma Indians and moved up the Gila to join the Pima Indians early in the nineteenth century.

The second group is composed of tribes living along the lower Colorado River. These tribes, the Cocopa, Yuma, Mohave, and the remnants of several related tribes, all speak languages belonging to the Yuman family. Their life is closely tied to the river which provides them with fish and floods their corn fields.

To the north and east of these are the members of the third group—the Walapai, Havasupai, and Yavapai, all linguistic cousins of the lower Colorado River people, and the Chemehuevi, Southern Paiute, and Ute, distant linguistic relatives of the Hopi.

To the south, in northern Mexico, within the area of the modern states of Chihuahua and Sonora, are half a dozen other tribes—Mayo, Yaqui, Opata, Seri, Tarahumare. Most of these are culturally and linguistically related to the southern and western Arizona farmers. However, since these tribes all live outside the boundaries of the present study, we will not discuss them further.

Like the Pueblo Indians, the Pima and Papago have a long history reaching far back into prehistory. It is probable, although not yet proved to the satisfaction of all archaeologists, that these two tribes are the descendants of the prehistoric Hohokam people. We do know that the Pima and Papago were living in what had been Hohokam territory when they were first discovered by Spanish explorers. And they were living much the same kind of lives as had the Hohokam people.

Physically and linguistically, the Pima and Papago are very much alike. They are also quite similar in many of their customs. What differences that exist between the two cultures are largely owing to differences in their environment. The Pima had the advantage of living along the Gila River, where they had ready access to water. The Papagos, however, mainly lived out in the southwestern Arizona Desert, where there was little water and where they had to depend to a much greater extent on the plant and animal resources of the country. Thus the Papago became known as the Desert People or the Bean People (because of eating wild mesquite beans), while the Pima were often called the River Dwellers.

Living in country that is warm and dry for the greater part of the year, the Pima and Papago had little need for solidly built masonry houses like those of the Pueblos. Formerly, their houses consisted of a framework of four posts surrounded by a circle of willow poles bent over and tied at the top. When this was covered with brush and grass and a layer of dirt, it formed a circular dome-shaped dwelling, with a low and fairly narrow opening left in one side for the doorway.

Today such houses are rarities. Most Pimas and Papagos live in rectangular, Mexican-style houses of one or two or three rooms, with walls built of adobe bricks or of a frame of upright poles plastered inside and out with adobe mud. Hard-packed dirt floors can still be found, but wooden or cement floors are becoming more and more common. Next to the houses are shaded work areas, called ramadas, consisting simply of a pole and brush roof supported on four posts, without side walls. Under these light and airy ramadas the entire family eats and sleeps and works during the hot summer months.

Houses are often more widely scattered in Papago communities, whereas houses in Pima villages tend to huddle much closer together.

Nor was much clothing needed in this warm desert country. In former times Pima and Papago men wore cotton or buckskin breechcloths and sandals, the women wraparound skirts or kilts of the same materials. Rawhide moccasins replaced sandals on long trips, and blankets were added in cooler weather. Both men and women left the hair long, and painted or sometimes tattooed the face and often the body as well. Now the men have adopted the white man's clothing, usually shirt and Levi's, and the women wear full skirts and blouses.

Both the Pima and Papago were farmers. But the Pima, living as they did along the banks of the Gila River, the only important stream in southern Arizona, had by far the best of it. Following in the footsteps of their probable ancestors, the Hohokam, they used the water from the river to irrigate their fields by means of a highly complex system of canals and ditches. They cultivated crops of corn, beans, squash, and cotton, later acquiring wheat and alfalfa and other products from the Spaniards.

The Papago had to work a lot harder to make a living. Their desert lands include some of the hottest and driest parts of the Southwest. To stay alive, the Papago were forced to shift their homes several times a year. In summer they lived in the flat country where their fields could be watered by floods pouring out of washes. After the summer rains stopped and the shallow waterholes dried up, the people moved to villages located near springs in the mountains. Each field camp had its own foothill camp where its residents kept duplicates of objects difficult to transport long distances, including such items as metates and manos and water jars and house posts.

To the Pima, hunting and gathering merely supplemented their usual diet of corn and beans and squash. They were important only in times of drought. But to the

Papago, hunting and gathering made the difference between life or starvation. Wild plant and animal foods furnished, in fact, well over half their food supply.

While the men hunted deer, antelope, mountain sheep, jackrabbits, packrats, and any other animals they came across, the women gathered mesquite beans, wild potato roots, and wild grass seeds. Even the many varieties of cacti weren't overlooked. They harvested the buds and fruits of most of these, particularly the fruits of the prickly pear and the giant sahuaro cactus.

Even so, in early times, many Papagos, instead of staying at their foothill villages, went to work for their richer cousins along the Gila River. Others wandered from the Pima villages to the Yumas and down into Mexico, trading their goods and their labor for enough to support themselves and their families until the wet season came again to the desert.

Both the Pima and Papago had patrilineal clans, where descent was traced through the father. But these clans seem to have had very little connection with either ceremonies or politics. These two tribes were also each divided into two moieties, called the Buzzard or Red Ant People and the Coyote or White Ant People. Like their clans, however, these groups seem to have had little influence on marriage or other customs.

Although the Pima formerly had a fairly strong tribal organization, the real political unit in both groups was the village. Actually, most Papago villages were politically independent. Village chiefs presided over a council of elders. In addition to the headman or village chief, each village also had a village crier, a keeper of the smoke (the main ceremonial official in each village), and other village officers who were in charge of certain ceremonies and festivals.

97

During times of war, Pima and Papago war parties were led by men selected for their fighting ability and leadership. Both tribes fought against Apache bands to the east, while the Pima also warred against the Yuma, Mohave, and Yavapai Indians in the west and north. For fear of the enemy's ghost, men who had killed an enemy in battle had to remain in quarantine outside the village for a period of sixteen days while an extensive ceremony of purification was carried out.

Ceremonies and rituals were neither as frequent nor as elaborate and colorful as those of the Pueblos. Religious practices largely centered on attempts to ensure an abundant food supply. One of the important Papago ceremonials was a rain ceremony, held in early summer after the ripening and gathering of the fruits of the giant cactus. Another important Papago ceremony was a deer dance, which took place in the autumn or early winter when the people had moved back to their foothill villages. The Papago also made ritual trips for salt to the shores of the Gulf of California, praying for the rain to follow them home.

Every four years both the Papago and Pima celebrated an important harvest festival, called the Vikita, or Wikita, during which sacred clowns and masked dancers performed.

8

The Colorado River Farmers

ALONG the lower Colorado River Valley, from the Gulf of California northward to what is now Hoover Dam, lived a number of Indian tribes who were also farmers. Like the Papago, however, most of them were only part-time farmers.

Although the basic culture was much the same throughout the desert country of southern and western Arizona, here in this river bottom country along the Colorado River its Yuman-speaking peoples had developed a distinctive manner of life, sharing features of culture from both southern California and southern Arizona.

Like the Pimas and Papagos, these Colorado River Indians didn't get much attention from the early Spanish explorers. In 1540, as a part of the Coronado expedition, Hernando de Alarcón by water and Melchior Diaz by land explored the lower Colorado River Valley and discovered some of its numerous Indian inhabitants. The next expedition was that of Juan de Oñate, the first governor of New Mexico, in 1604 and 1605. Nearly a hundred years passed before Europeans again visited that area, since they weren't too interested in this hot desert country. In 1701 and 1702 a Jesuit priest, Eusebio Kino, made two visits to the lower Colorado River tribes. During the following three-quarters of a century several other missionaries reached the Colorado River. But none of these short visits made any lasting impression on the Indians.

However, the establishment of Spanish missions and settlements in California, beginning in 1769, changed the picture. Although the Spaniards had originally reached California by water, by way of the Pacific Ocean, they were anxious to establish land communication between these new missions and the Spanish missions and towns in northern Sonora. Such a route was opened up by Juan Bautista de Anza and Fray Francisco Garcés in 1774 and 1775. By 1780 Garcés had even established two missions along the Colorado River in the vicinity of the present town of Yuma, Arizona. These missions didn't last too long, however, as trouble with the Indians developed almost at once. To these people, the setting up of missions in their territory meant gifts of trinkets and tobacco. When the presents didn't materialize, the Indians revolted in July, 1781, and killed more than thirty Spanish soldiers, along with Fray Garcés and three other friars.

For nearly three centuries all of the exploring in the Southwest had been done by Europeans, chiefly Spaniards, coming up from the south, from Mexico. But the opening of the nineteenth century saw a change. With the Louisiana Purchase in 1803, the United States began to develop its own explorers. Traders and adventurers from St. Louis and points east found their way to

Santa Fe. Within a short time the search for beaver skins to make hats brought trappers to the Gila and Colorado rivers.

Then the United States fought with Mexico, and Arizona and New Mexico and California became American. More and more Americans began pouring into the area. Some kept on to California, but many stayed in the Southwest.

Both the Pimas and Papagos were friendly and peaceful, never fighting with the Spaniards and later Americans who invaded and took over much of their former territory. The Pimas were, in fact, of great help to the American pioneers crossing southern Arizona during the California gold rush. But, as we shall see, most of the Yuman tribes were much more warlike and frequently fought against the Spaniards and later Americans.

Until the coming of the Spaniards, these Colorado River Yumans—the Cocopa, Yuma, Mohave, Halchidhoma, Kohuana, Halyikwamai, and Kaveltcadom—lived in scattered settlements along the banks of the Colorado River.

These Colorado River tribes were much alike in looks and speech and culture. They were remarkable for their huge size, many of them being over 6 feet in height. Most of them were also remarkable for their happy, sunny, carefree natures.

The Colorado River forms a winding, ribbonlike green oasis in the midst of a hot and dry desert. Summers are hot and winters are warm, with only occasional cool days and even fewer rainy ones.

Like their probable Patayan ancestors, these Yuman-speaking Indians were farmers. Their principal crops were the usual trio grown by the agricultural tribes of native North America—maize or corn, beans, and squash or pumpkins. The Mohave Indians also grew sunflowers. Most of their corn was of the white variety, although, like other peoples of the Southwest, they also grew ears with colored kernels. During historic times they added melons and wheat to this list.

Yet these Indians were indifferent farmers. They practiced little or no irrigation. The Colorado River was too big to fool around with by trying to dam it or by digging ditches or canals. They farmed the narrow strip of bottom land fringing the river. For water they depended entirely upon the annual flooding of their fields

Yuma Indian house on the Yuma Indian Reservation, California.
(Bureau of Indian Affairs)

in May and June by the Colorado, swollen by melting snow and rain far to the northeast in the river's Rocky Mountain headwaters in Colorado, Utah, and Wyoming. These floodwaters left a coating of rich silt spread out over the valley land. In this moisture-laden soil, with plenty of warm sunshine every day, plants grew fast. Outside of occasional weeding with a mesquite wood hoe, they needed and received little attention.

The Indians supplemented their domestic crops with wild plants which flourished abundantly along the flats bordering the Colorado River. Of primary importance were the beanlike pods of mesquite trees.

Although big game was scarce in the valley, the Indians hunted such small game as rabbits, wood rats, squirrels, muskrats, beavers, badgers, and raccoons.

But fish more than made up for their lack of meat. Fish were plentiful in the muddy waters of the Colorado River. Soft, bony, and more or less tasteless (at least to most of us today), these squawfish, humpbacked suckers, and bony tails were relished by the Mohave and other Colorado River Indians. Many fish were caught with nets or large seines. Often fish were dipped out of the water with basketry scoops or were caught by hand in the shallow water of ponds or in holes along the riverbank.

Although fish were sometimes broiled, they were more often cooked in the form of a stew, with head, tail, scales, bones, and all being included, either with or without cornmeal or other ingredients.

Living in a hot and dry country, these Indians could get along for most of the year with open-sided, flat-topped shelters or ramadas. The pole and arrowweed roof not only furnished shade but also served as a convenient storage place for food.

103

Like the Pimas and Papagos, the Colorado River Indians didn't have good building stones handy and had to settle for houses made of poles and brush and mud. Their winter houses looked something like those of the Pimas, earth-covered pole-and-brush structures with sloping sides, with a low doorway that could be covered by a bark mat. Although each family usually had its own winter house, prominent and influential men sometimes built larger brush and mud houses where all their relatives and friends could sleep on cold winter nights.

To store mesquite beans and other foods, they built cylindrical bins of interlaced bundles of arrowweed plastered with mud on a platform raised 4 or 5 feet above the ground.

With even warmer weather than the Pimas and Papagos had, these Colorado River Indians had little need for clothing. Everyday wear was scanty. Most men formerly wore nothing at all. Later they put on a breechcloth woven from willow bark. At home they went barefoot, putting on sandals only when traveling. Women wore two small willow-bark aprons, one in front and one in back. For cold weather, they added a rabbit-skin blanket. Many Indians also carried a burning torch or firebrand in the hand to help keep them warm.

Both men and women wore their hair long, hanging to the waist in back and in bangs over the forehead. While women let their hair hang loosely, men twisted their hair into a number of long, pencillike strands.

What these Indians lacked in the way of clothing, however, they more than made up for in paint. Tattooing was universal. Bars, dots, and lines were tattooed on the faces of both men and women. Red, black, blue, and white paint was also used freely on both the face and the body.

Although the Mohave Indians were a river people, they had no canoes. Along with other Colorado River Yumans, they were great swimmers. When they wanted to cross the river, they usually swam across. Sometimes they used a floating log as a swimming aid. And sometimes they straddled a log and floated downstream. They also built crude rafts of bundles of tules held together with wooden pins.

Each of the Colorado River tribes looked on itself as a unit. Each thought of its land as a country with definite localities. Settlements were small and scattered, uniformly grouped into clusters of houses of friends and relatives. You could hardly call them villages, at least not in the sense of Pima or Papago villages.

Even though little formal government existed, the Mohave and other Colorado River tribes showed a strong sense of tribal solidarity. Although the tribe had no tribal council, it did have a tribal chief who had, however, few duties and little authority.

The Mohave shared with other Yuman tribes of the Colorado River Valley a peculiar clan system. Membership in one of the twenty or more clans (kinship divisions) was through the father's side of the family. Yet, oddly, only the women bore the clan name. Within these clans marriage was prohibited. But this was almost the only function that clans had. They had, for example, nothing to do with the religious activities of the tribe.

Warfare was one of the most distinctive features of the life of these Yuman-speaking tribes. Wars were not fought, however, for economic gain or territorial conquest. War honors were important, and good fighters won high prestige in the tribe. Although they fought with such outside tribes as the Pima and Papago and Southern Paiute, most of their fighting was with other

105

Yuman-speaking tribes along the Colorado and Gila rivers. The Mohave and Yuma, for example, were usually allied against the Maricopa, Halchidhoma, and Cocopa tribes. To escape such attacks, the Maricopas moved farther and farther up the Gila River, finally joining the Pimas in the nineteenth century. The Kohuana and Halyikwamai, after suffering heavy losses, were finally absorbed by the Maricopa. Both the Halchidhoma and Kaveltcadom groups also took refuge with the Maricopas on the Gila River.

Military activities of these Colorado River tribes usually involved fairly large numbers of people, from fifty to a hundred or more. For long-range fighting the Indians used bows and arrows with sharpened wooden tips. But they preferred to fight at close quarters with mallet-headed "potato masher" clubs of mesquite wood and longer straight clubs of screw-bean wood used for cracking skulls.

Fighting sometimes took on a highly formalized character, with arranged pitched battles between warriors drawn up in opposing ranks, challenges, where war leaders would exchange insults and brandish their clubs at each other, and even combats between single warriors.

The only prisoners taken during raids were girls and young women. A scalp dance was held within a day or two after the return of a war party.

The Mohave, like other Yuman tribes, believed that dreams were basic to everything in life. This is the dominating feature of Yuman religion. Shamans (medicine men), singers, funeral orators, chiefs, and war leaders were all thought to get their power from dreams.

The shamans were influential people. These professional medicine men not only cured and bewitched people but also predicted the weather, located enemies,

Cremation ceremony for a Mohave chief.
(Southwest Museum)

foretold the outcome of battles, and discovered lost or stolen articles.

Ceremonialism and dancing were largely undeveloped among these people. Taking their place was the singing of long and elaborate myth songs and song cycles.

Death furnished the occasion for their most elaborate rituals. When an individual was on his deathbed, his relatives and friends began singing songs and making ceremonial speeches in his honor. If the sick man rallied, the singing might go on for two or three days. Meanwhile a funeral pyre was prepared near the house by scooping a shallow trench in the sand and piling willows and cottonwood logs in it. As soon as the patient died, the body was laid on the logs and cremated, along with the belongings of the deceased. While the fire was blazing, the shouts and lamentations of relatives and friends were at a peak. Mourners often threw on the fire their own personal belongings, even stripping off their clothing. When the fire had burned out, sand was pushed over it to wipe out all traces of the cremation. The dead man's house and shade and granaries were also burned, and the crops in his fields were destroyed or given away. The deceased's family also moved, temporarily at least, to another locality.

For four days following the cremation, the mourning relatives drank no cold water and ate no salt or meat or fish. Mourners had to cut their hair, females to ear level, males to shoulder length. Along with the mourners, everyone who had touched or taken care of the corpse or who had made a speech had to go through a purification ritual.

These Indians believed that the dead person's soul stayed in the neighborhood of his former home for four days and nights. Then it traveled on downstream to the south to the land of the dead. If the dead person had not been tattooed, however, he couldn't enter the land of the dead but had to go down a rodent's hole.

To the Colorado Indians illness was thought of as being caused by the sick person's soul having been either taken away or affected by some injury or shock or by sorcerers or ghosts. The shaman was assumed to be able to cause sickness as well as to heal it. In curing, the shaman, or medicine man, used singing, the laying on of hands, and blowing a spray of saliva. As was often the case in other tribes, a medicine man who had too many patients die was accused of bewitching them and was killed by their relatives.

Although some men had more than one wife, marriages were generally monogamous. A married couple went to live with the husband's parents. You might say that marriage was casual, involving neither wedding ceremony nor gift exchange. Divorce was equally casual and common.

9

Northern Hunters and Gatherers

IN THE DESERT and plateau country of northwestern Arizona, eastern California, and southern Nevada and Utah and Colorado lived our third group of Southwestern desert dwellers. Of its half dozen Indian tribes, the Yavapai formerly ranged over west-central Arizona from the Colorado to the Verde River. To the north were the Walapai and Havasupai, the Walapai in northwestern Arizona south of the great bend of the Colorado River and the Havasupai to the east in Cataract Canyon, a side branch of the Grand Canyon. Still farther north and west were the other three tribes, the Utes in Colorado and Utah, the Southern Paiutes in southwestern Utah, northwestern Arizona, and southern Nevada, and the Chemehuevi in California in the eastern half of the Mohave Desert south of Death Valley.

The first three of these tribes, the Walapai, Havasupai, and Yavapai, were close linguistic relatives of the downriver Yumans, the Mohave and Maricopa and the rest of the Yuman-speaking peoples. The other three tribes, the Chemehuevi, Southern Paiute, and Ute, were all Shoshonean speakers, distantly related to the Puebloan Hopi Indians.

The Walapai are named from a Yuman word meaning "Pine Tree People," while Havasupai signifies "People of the Blue Green Water," and Yavapai, "People of the Sun" or "Crooked Mouth People."

Nor were any of these tribes as numerous as their more sedentary relatives and neighbors. The Yavapai, for example, probably never numbered more than fifteen hundred. Yet they formerly roamed over a territory covering more than 20,000 square miles.

As happened with the tribes of southern and western Arizona, the few Spanish expeditions that penetrated into this area during the sixteenth, seventeenth, and eighteenth centuries left little impression of their passing. And only after 1860 did the Americans make any effort to settle there. Although most of these tribes fought against the Americans at one time or another, the Yavapais probably caused more trouble than all of the other tribes combined. In fact, the Yavapais were, and still are, often miscalled Mohave-Apaches or Yuma-Apaches or Yavapai-Apaches.

None of these Indians lived like their linguistic cousins, the lower river Yumans and the Puebloan Hopi. In fact, many of them, particularly the Walapai, Havasupai, Yavapai, and some of the Southern Paiutes, have remained closer to the ancient Desert Culture than any other tribes in the Southwest.

With the exception of the Havasupai, all of these tribes, like their probable Desert Culture ancestors, were primarily hunters and gatherers. Throughout much of their area both water and food were scarce. To get

111

enough to eat and drink, they had to move with the seasons from the lowlands to the highlands and back again, following game and ripening plants. Since food and water in any one place were generally sufficient to support only a limited number of people for a limited period of time, they usually roamed about in small bands or family groups.

Some Yavapai bands, for example, ranged far from their home localities, the distance of their range depending largely upon the places where food and water were to be had in that particular season and year. Moving on foot, with few belongings to weigh them down, they frequently covered from 20 to 30 miles per day. In emergencies, these Indians have been known to travel on foot 50 miles in a single day.

While the men hunted deer, antelope, mountain sheep, badgers, raccoons, rabbits, wood rats, squirrels, skunks, caterpillars, and almost anything else that was alive, the women gathered mesquite beans, acorns, pinyon nuts, walnuts, mescal, cactus fruits, and a wide variety of greens and seeds and roots and berries. Unlike the Colorado River Yumans, the Yavapai and most of their neighbors wouldn't eat fish.

Given these circumstances, you can understand why few of these tribes were ever able to accumulate enough surplus food to store against a rainy day.

As we mentioned earlier, the Havasupai tribe was the exception to this hunting and gathering way of life. The Havasupai, who appear to be an offshoot of the Walapai (their speech is nearly identical), seemingly picked up a knowledge of farming and irrigation from their Hopi neighbors to the east. Settling in the green valley of Cataract Canyon, they were able to irrigate their small fields of corn, beans, and squash with the waters of Cataract Creek. But they were only part-time farmers. After the October harvest, they would climb out of the canyon and camp among the pinyon and juniper trees on the plateau, supplementing their farm produce by hunting and gathering in typical Walapai fashion.

The Walapai also farmed wherever they could. But their country was poor, and good land was limited to a few small patches near springs and streams. Consequently they remained essentially hunters and gatherers, using their meager farm crops to furnish them with a yearly feast or two. Some of the Yavapai living along the Colorado River adopted the use of houses and farming from the Yuma and Mohave Indians. But, like the Walapai, the Yavapai were not farmers at heart and relied mainly on hunting and gathering for their subsistence.

The Chemehuevi and Southern Paiute also occasionally farmed small patches of land where they could find them. But in the main they lived on what their environment provided—deer, rats, rabbits, lizards, seeds, mescal, and mesquite beans.

Actually, the Chemehuevi are probably an offshoot of the Southern Paiutes who moved into the Mohave Desert at some remote time in the past. Shortly after the Yuma and Mohave Indians drove the last of the Halchidhomas and Kohuanas out of the Colorado Valley, the Chemehuevis left their desert homes and moved into the greener and far richer valley. There they began to live like their Mohave neighbors.

As you might expect, all of these tribes were characterized by the great simplicity of their way of life. They were a lot poorer in the material things of life than were their neighboring relatives, the sedentary Hopis and

113

Colorado River Yumans. With a migratory hunting and gathering pattern of living, they had few permanent houses and no large villages. More often than not, their houses were small temporary shelters of poles and branches and brush, sometimes covered with skins, sometimes with mud. The Walapai, for example, usually built a dome-shaped hut of poles and branches laid over a four-post foundation and covered with juniper bark or thatch. The Walapai also built flimsy summer shelters of branches as protection against the sun. Yavapai huts, commonly called wickiups, were small temporary circular shelters, usually newly made at each camping place out of branches and brush and mud. At times some groups took shelter in natural caves.

Living in a higher and cooler country, these plateau Indians seldom if ever went nude as did the lower Colorado River Yumans. Clothing was generally made of buckskin or of bark fiber, the latter more common in areas where deer were scarce. Men wore breechcloths of buckskin or bark and buckskin moccasins or fiber sandals, while women wore wraparound bark skirts or front and back aprons of buckskin or bark. In colder weather they added rabbit-skin blankets. Rabbit-skin robes were also used as beds or sleeping blankets.

A few of these tribes, such as the Walapai and Southern Paiutes, made a little pottery, mainly for cooking and the storage of water. But all of them made baskets. Baskets or bags of some kind were almost a necessity for nomadic seed gatherers. The Walapai, for instance, made wickerwork seed beaters, large conical seed gathering and carrying baskets, and flat basketry trays for winnowing and parching seeds. The Walapai also made water bottles by coating the inside and outside of tall, narrow-necked baskets with pitch.

114

Social and political organization among most of these upland tribes was also relatively simple. Because of the limitations of the poor environment over much of the area, large groups of people could not stay together for any length of time. Small family groups cr bands tended to wander over large areas in search of food. The family was the sole social unit. Clans were absent in this area. The one exception to this occurred among the south-eastern Yavapai, who had matrilineal clans, presumably as a result of influence from the neighboring Western Apaches.

There was no formal wedding ceremony and no exchange of gifts, although the prospective bridegroom might bring a deer or other gifts to the girl's father. Divorce was just as informal.

These upland Yumans and Shoshoneans were loosely organized politically. Most tribes, such as the Yavapai, were divided into a number of bands, each composed of a number of extended families. Each band had its chief and sometimes even two or more chiefs. The authority of these chiefs was so limited, however, that they might be called advisers rather than chiefs.

There were few organized religious rituals or ceremonies. Native religious beliefs and practices were extremely simple. The shaman, or medicine man, who acquired his power through dreams, was the only religious practitioner. The shaman was also the local doctor, performing during curing rites. A shaman was often more feared than respected, as he was suspected of causing disease. The badge of a shaman's office was his gourd rattle, which he shook while he sang over his patients. And if he lost too many patients, he was apt to lose his own life at the hands of friends or relatives of the deceased.

The Walapai looked on the Hopi, Havasupai, and Navaho Indians as friends. The Mohave, too, were regarded as friends, although there were occasional battles between them. The Paiutes also were troublesome at times. But the Yavapai were their chief enemies, raiding the Walapai almost yearly.

10

Apache and Navaho Raiders

FIVE APACHE TRIBES, including their close relatives the Navaho, form the last major group of Southwestern Indians. Unlike the Pueblo and Pima Indians and all the members of the other groups, the Apache Indians are not old settlers.

When and how the Apaches and Navahos arrived in the Southwest are still questions without definite answers. As we mentioned in Chapter 5, we do know that these Athabascan-speaking Indians migrated southward from their ancestral home in northwestern Canada. Spanish documents tell us that there were Apaches in the Southwest as early as the late sixteenth and early seventeenth centuries. So do tree-ring studies made on wooden posts from old Navaho houses. They may have been there still earlier. We just don't know.

Although there are actually seven of these southern Athabascan-speaking Indian tribes, we can forget about the Lipan and Kiowa Apaches since they were more closely allied culturally with the Plains than they were with the Southwest.

Of the five remaining Apache tribes, the Navaho lived in northeastern New Mexico and northeastern Arizona, the Western Apache in eastern Arizona, the Chiricahua Apache in southeastern Arizona, southwestern New Mexico, and northern Mexico, the Mescalero Apache in south-central New Mexico east of the Rio Grande, and the Jicarilla Apache in northeastern New Mexico and southeastern Colorado.

The history of the Apaches and Navahos is almost a history of warfare in the Southwest. From the time we first read about these Indians in Spanish records until they were finally subdued by the United States Army, the Navahos and Apaches were warlike. They had to be to survive. The Spaniards were always on the lookout for cheap labor to work their mines and fields. What could be cheaper than an Indian slave, preferably a Navaho or Apache slave? To this, the Indians retaliated in the only way they knew—by raiding Spaniards and Mexicans and even Pueblos and Pimas and other settled Indian groups. In 1776, for example, the Apaches almost completely destroyed the town of Magdalena, Mexico. Raiding for plunder became a fixed part of the Apache and Navaho way of life.

When the United States took over the Southwest in the middle of the nineteenth century, the Mexican authorities were happy to turn over the problem of the Apaches and Navahos to the Americans. The Indians were also happy, thinking that the White-Eyes, as they called these light-eyed newcomers, would chase out the hated Mexicans and life would be better. But they were quickly disillusioned. The Mexicans stayed, and the White-Eyes kept coming in greater and greater numbers,

118

crowding in closer and closer to the ancient Indian hunting and camping grounds and killing off the deer and elk and other animals.

For the next few decades the United States Army had its hands full trying to handle the Navahos and Apaches. This was understandable. Of all the American Indians, the Chiricahuas and Western Apaches were probably the greatest all-around fighters. And the Navahos and Mescalero Apaches weren't too far behind. These Indians were excellent hit-and-run fighters. Man for man they were a match for the best troops that the United States Army could send against them. But they couldn't hold out forever against superior numbers and superior equipment.

The Mescaleros were the first to be rounded up. Then the Army went after the Navahos. In 1863, Kit Carson led an expedition into the heart of the Navaho country. Not being able to catch up with the Indians, Carson and the soldiers killed their sheep, burned their cornfields, and cut down their peach trees. For the Navahos, the choice was either starve or surrender, and most of them chose surrender. More than eight thousand of them were taken to Bosque Redondo, Fort Sumner, New Mexico— "the Long Walk," as the Navahos ever after called it. Four years of captivity were all the Navahos could stand. After signing a treaty promising never to fight again, they were finally permitted to return to their own country.

Now the United States Army could turn all its attention to the Chiricahuas and Western Apaches. But this was no easy task, particularly in the case of the Chiricahuas. For this was the tribe that spawned such famous chiefs and medicine men as Cochise, Nana, Mangas Coloradas, Victorio, Naiche, Loco, and Geronimo. Off and on for nearly twenty years, this one small tribe of

A western Apache village of wickiups in Arizona's White Mountains.

(Tad Nichols)

barely a thousand Indians led thousands of soldiers of both the United States Army and the Mexican Army on a merry and bloody chase from Arizona to Old Mexico to New Mexico to Arizona and back again. Not until 1886 were the last of the Chiricahuas rounded up and shipped off to prison in Florida, bringing to an end one of the most colorful eras in Southwestern history.

These Southwestern Athabascan tribes didn't call themselves Apaches or Navahos. They spoke of themselves as Dine, "the People." They were not, however, as close in material culture and economy as the Pueblo peoples. The Navaho and Western Apache tribes shared a basically similar way of life. Yet each differed in many ways from the other and differed still further from the Chiricahua and Mescalero and Jicarilla Apaches.

Their social and political organization had one thing in common: None of them had a central tribal organization. Neither the Chiricahuas nor the Western Apaches, for example, were a single, united tribe. Nor did they think of themselves as such. The Chiricahuas were divided into three separate and distinct bands, while the Western Apaches had five such groups. So did the Mescalero Apaches. Each band was again broken down into a number of local groups, each of these being composed of from ten to twenty or more households or extended families. It was actually this local group, not the band, that normally functioned as the basic social, economic, and military body. This was the largest group that had a definite leader, who held his position through a combination of personal magnetism and proven experience. If an entire band ever got together for any purpose, the strongest of the local headmen served as chief of the band. Only rarely did this happen, however, since the local groups, particularly among the Chiricahuas, were too thinly scattered over a wide desert and mountain area to get together very often.

Economically, most of these Apache tribes made their living by hunting and gathering and by raiding. The Navahos and Western Apaches did, however, adopt farming from the Pueblo Indians, probably not long after they reached the Southwest. So did some Jicarilla

Apaches. But all of them still depended to a considerable extent upon hunting deer, antelope, rabbits, and other wild game, and upon the gathering of cactus fruit, pinyon nuts, mesquite beans, mescal heads, and other wild plant foods. The Mescalero Apaches, in fact, seem to have acquired their name because of their staple food, mescal.

Mescal, the agave or century plant so widespread over the Southwest, was a favorite and important food not only of most Apaches but also of Paiutes and Walapais and Yavapais and many other Indians. Most Indians usually cooked mescal in large quantities, drying and storing the surplus against a rainy day. To do this, they cut the hearts or crowns out of the center of the plants by means of sharp stones or equally sharp, chisel-shaped sticks. To cook the mescal heads, the Indians dug huge pits from 10 to 20 feet in diameter and from 3 to 5 feet deep. After lining the hole with rocks, they filled it with wood, covered the wood with more rocks, and set the pile afire. When the fire burned down, the mescal heads were piled on top of the hot rocks and covered over with wet grass and brush and dirt. The mescal heads were left to bake in this steamy fireless cooker for a day or two. The baked mescal could then be eaten as it was or could be cut up and dried and stored away.

Old and long-abandoned mescal pits like this have been found all over the Southwest, from Utah to Mexico and from Nevada eastward across Arizona into New Mexico and Texas. There are literally dozens of them in and around the Grand Canyon of the Colorado River.

To most Apaches, particularly after they began to acquire horses, raiding was a recognized and necessary part of their economy. They were looking for loot, not glory. On their raids against Mexicans and Pueblos and other Indians, they stole anything they could lay their hands on—food, clothing, horses, cattle, mules, and women and children. Horses and cattle and other goods that were picked up in Mexico were frequently traded to Mexicans and Indians in northern Arizona and New Mexico, while livestock stolen in the north might wind up hundreds of miles to the south in Mexico. Between 1846 and 1850, for example, the Navahos stole 7,000 horses, over 12,000 mules, 31,000 cattle, and 450,000 sheep from the Rio Grande villages alone. No telling how much more they stole from other places. And the Chiricahuas and Western Apaches were even greater raiders than the Navahos. Without the plunder garnered on raids many Apaches would have starved.

Horses came in handy on raids, to get from one place to another in a hurry. But the Apaches preferred to fight on foot. They could and often did cover 40 to 50 miles a day on foot. As a matter of fact, the Chiricahuas and Western Apaches were not the horsemen that their relatives on the Plains were. Often they rode their horses until the animals dropped dead. Then the Indians would cook and eat them and start looking for more horses. Given the choice, many Apaches would eat mule, horse, or burro meat before that of cattle or sheep.

Since so many of these Indians had to be on the move much of the time, either hunting and gathering or raiding, few of them ever got around to developing permanent homes. Most of the Jicarilla and Mescalero Apaches lived in skin tipis similar to those of the Plains Indians. The Chiricahua and Western Apache home was the wickiup, a large, domed framework of poles and brush covered with layers of bear grass overlapping like thatch. In rainy weather and in wintertime the wickiup

Rectangular Navaho hogan built of stone in western New Mexico.
(Bureau of Indian Affairs)

used to be covered with skins. Now the Indians use canvas or cloth. The doorway, a low rectangular opening, usually faced to the east.

Most Navaho houses, called hogans, blend so well into the landscape that you can drive past a dozen and spot only two or three of them. Their earliest type of dwelling was a forked-stick hogan. Over three upright forked cedar poles forming the foundation, other poles were laid; the whole was plastered with mud and earth. To this they added a covered doorway which projected out a little toward the east, as dictated by their mythology. In addition to this ancient and traditional house, the Navahos also constructed several other styles. Most of these were circular, windowless, six- or eight-sided houses of horizontally laid logs. The upper tiers of logs were gradually built in toward the center, like cribwork, to form a dome-shaped roof which was covered with packed earth. Today many houses are built of stone, either circular or square to rectangular in shape. Some even have glass windows.

Unlike most tribes, the Navahos do not live in villages. Many families move with the seasons, following their sheep in search of greener pastures. For this reason, most families have two or three hogans, located in widely scattered areas and occupied at different times of the year.

Near each Navaho hogan are other structures—a brush or stone corral, a dugout or two for storage, and a flat-topped, brush-covered ramada or shade, beneath which much of the household work is carried on. Off to one side is the sweat lodge, a smaller copy of the old, mud-plastered, forked-stick hogan. In warm weather kitchen, workshop, bedroom, and nursery may all be found under the shade of a cottonwood tree.

Navaho and Apache clothing was formerly made almost entirely of buckskin—breechcloth and a shirt and a pair of thigh-high moccasins for the men (Navaho men, however, wore low-cut moccasins), and a shirt and skirt and moccasins for the women. Apache men wore their hair long and unbraided and tied strips of buckskin (later cloth) around the head to keep the hair out of

Navaho hogan, ramada, sweat lodge, and corral.
(Tad Nichols)

their eyes. Navaho men tied their long hair in a compact club at the back in imitation of the Pueblo Indian style of hairdressing. After the Indians began to get cloth from the Mexicans and later Americans, the Apaches wore loosely fitting shirts of cotton or calico, which hung down over a pair of loose cotton drawers. Today both

Apache and Navaho men usually wear blue-denim pants, western-style shirts, broad-brimmed hats, and either cowboy boots or work shoes.

By the 1870's Apache women were beginning to copy the styles of white women's dresses they saw on military posts. This long, voluminous skirt, made of 10 to 20 yards of brightly colored calico, and topped by an equally bright calico blouse, is still popular with many Apache women. The dress of Navaho women is similar, consisting of full-flounced skirts of calico or sateen and bright blouses of velveteen.

Older Apache women tended to wear their hair hanging loosely, while the younger ones usually parted the hair in the middle, drawing it together in the back and wrapping it in a knot. Many Navaho women followed the same practice.

Most Apaches and Navahos spent most of their lives in the company of their relatives. Like the Hopis and Zunis, Navahos and Western Apaches traced descent through the mother. Also like the Hopis and Zunis, residence was matrilocal, a married couple usually building their hogan or wickiup near that of the wife's mother. The basic Apache or Navaho camp cluster was the extended family, consisting of a woman and her husband and unmarried children, together with her married daughters and their husbands and unmarried children. Married sons, of course, were not included in this extended family since they normally lived near the families of their wives.

Each household within a family camp was a self-contained unit, having its own hogan or wickiup, eating at its own fire, and so on. But most other activities—farming, hunting, gathering, raiding, house building—were shared by two or three households or by the entire extended family.

In addition to membership in an extended family each Navaho and Western Apache belonged to a clan. The other tribes of Apaches didn't have clans. But the Navahos adopted the idea of clans from the Pueblo Indians, and the Western Apaches either adopted it from the Pueblo Indians or from the Navahos. Every Navaho and Western Apache boy or girl was born into one clan, the clan of his or her mother, and remained a member of that clan as long as he or she lived. There were some sixty of these clans in each tribe. Each clan had a name, usually that of some locality. Navaho clans, for instance, bore such names as Poles-Strung-Out, Mud, Bitter-Water, Yucca-Blossom-Patch, Red-House, and Grey-Earth-Place. One of the chief functions of the clan was to regulate marriage—marriage, of course, being prohibited between members of the same or related clans, because every member of an individual's clan was considered a relative. Western Apache clans also controlled farming sites and rights to ceremonials and furnished the basis for organization of war parties.

Marriage was looked on as the normal state of affairs by both Navahos and Apaches. Failure to get married was extremely rare and, in fact, considered abnormal.

Beyond preliminary marriage negotiations and an exchange of gifts between the two families, an Apache couple began their married life without benefit of ceremony. Navahos, however, held a wedding ceremony at the hogan of the bride's parents. The young couple ate cornmeal mush from a wedding basket. (This was a special basket of distinctive design usually made for the Navahos by the Utes.) Following this, the wedding guests had a feast.

Since an Apache or Navaho spent most of his time in close contact with his relatives—his parents, brothers and sisters, grandparents, aunts and uncles, cousins of all kinds, and various and sundry in-laws, along with countless clan relatives—the manner in which he treated these relatives was highly important. A new husband was expected to work for his parents-in-law to help fill the economic gap made by their own sons marrying and moving away. He had to use special terms for different classes of relatives. Some he could joke with; others he had to treat with respect.

But above all, a Navaho or Apache man had to avoid his mother-in-law. He could not talk directly to her or look at her or be in the same room with her. Nor could the mother-in-law even see her daughter married. If any of these events did happen, supernatural powers would, or so the Navaho thought, strike them blind. This taboo wasn't easy for the two to keep. To get around a man and his mother-in-law seeing each other, the two houses were usually built so that the entrances were not in sight of each other. If a woman accidentally met her son-in-law, she would throw her blanket over her head and turn away. The man would also face the other way and hurry off in the opposite direction. If a woman wanted to visit her daughter's house and her son-in-law was still at home, she would send word so that the man could leave.

An Apache man also held his father-in-law in marked respect. Although they sometimes did speak directly to each other, frequently the father-in-law would tell his daughter what he wanted, even when he knew her husband was within hearing distance.

Some Apache and Navaho men even faced the problem of trying to avoid two or three or four mothers-in-law. But polygyny, the custom of having more than one wife, was not too common. The average man had all he could do to support one wife, and the practice was confined largely to wealthy individuals, to chiefs and sub-chiefs. Each of a man's wives and her children occupied a separate hogan or wickiup. Some Indians who wanted a second wife neatly sidestepped the difficulty of having two mothers-in-law by marrying sisters.

⚡ As in many tribes, divorce was simple among the Navahos and Apaches. Since the woman owned the house, all she had to do was stack her husband's belongings outside the door. When he returned and saw this, he knew what it meant and went home to his mother. If a man wanted a divorce, he might tell his wife he was going hunting and just not return. Either was free to remarry immediately. The husband of an unfaithful wife might whip her or he might cut off the tip of her nose or he might even kill her.

Both Apaches and Navahos shared a fear and horror of the dead and anything and everything connected with death. This fear rested on the dread of the ghosts (Navaho *chindi*) of the departed, who might return to harm the living. When a Navaho died inside a house, the body was taken out through a hole broken in the north wall of the hogan, always the direction of evil. The body was buried just as quickly as possible, either in the ground or in a crevice in the rock. The hogan or wickiup was abandoned and usually burned, along with the possessions of the dead, to prevent contamination. A dying Navaho was sometimes removed from the hogan so that he could die outside and thus spare the house. All the mourners, particularly those who had handled the corpse, had to observe elaborate precautions and purification rites to avoid contamination. The site where the death occurred was also abandoned, and the family moved to a new location. This might, however, not be more than a few hundred yards, from one side of a field or valley to the other side. The name of the dead person was taboo and no longer mentioned.

Apaches and Navahos were and still are deeply religious. Both believed in a host of supernatural beings who had power to harm or to help human beings. The Apache Mountain Spirits, or Gans, who were thought to inhabit the interior of certain mountains, corresponded to the Navaho Holy People. Changing Woman was the Navaho version of Apache White Painted Woman; and the Navaho Hero Twins, Monster Slayer and Child of the Waters, corresponded to the two culture heroes of the Apaches, Killer of Enemies and Child of the Water. Masked dancers impersonated or represented these Mountain Spirits and Holy People during certain Apache and Navaho ceremonies.

Both Apaches and Navahos believed in witches and ghosts. Even today many educated Navahos still believe in witchcraft. Almost all Navahos dislike going out alone at night, partly from fear of ghosts and partly from fear of witches. Ghosts, of course, were the evil spirits of the dead, who might return at any time to seek revenge for some fancied wrong or neglect. If a corpse had not been buried properly or if some of his personal property had not been put in the grave with him, the ghost would come back to his burial place or to his former hogan. Ghosts come out after dark, in human form or disguised as coyotes or owls or indefinite black objects. They might chase people or jump on them or throw dirt on them. Ghosts were to be feared not only in themselves, but as bearers of bad news.

Witches were bad men and women who were thought to have supernatural powers. Like ghosts, they operated chiefly at night, robbing graves, stealing property, and using spells and other ritual means to cause sickness or

131

Western Apache masked Gan dancers.

(Tad Nichols)

death. Navaho witches often wore the skins of wolves or other animals as disguises. Nearly all human ailments and disasters were believed to be due to supernatural causes—an attack by a ghost or witch or by some other supernatural force or power.

That's where the Apache or Navaho shaman, or medicine man, came into the picture. To effect a cure or to ward off a threatened disaster, it was necessary to have a ceremony or ritual. This could be done only by a shaman. Shamans were men, sometimes women, who were believed to have received power from a supernatural source, which gave them strength beyond their own resources. Through this power Apache medicine men, for example, could cure disease, ward off evil and sickness, prophesy future events, ensure success in hunting or in raids or in love, locate lost persons, find lost or hidden objects, and control the weather and other natural events.

Basic to both Apache and Navaho religion were their ceremonies and rituals. Most ceremonies were for the curing of disease. Diseases were accurately pigeonholed, and each had its own special ceremony.

Navaho curing ceremonies are much more complex than are those of the Apaches. There are more than fifty Navaho curing chants, each with numerous variations. The particular curing chant used depended on the nature of the disease or injury. Special diagnosticians were called in to determine the nature and cause of the trouble. Then the shaman, or medicine man, and his helpers tried to effect a cure through the proper chant.

Although these Navaho curing ceremonies followed a general pattern, no two were exactly alike. Some, like the Night Way Chant, were nine-day ceremonies; others were shorter. These chants were solemn and complicated rituals, involving elaborate ritual paraphernalia,

133

the singing of sacred songs, the recitation of religious poems up to several hundred verses in length, dances by masked dancers impersonating the Holy People, the making of sand paintings, the use of emetics, the sprinkling of pollen, the ritual blowing of breath, sweat baths, all-night sings, and symbolic offerings.

The particular ceremony chosen depended also upon the ability of a family to pay. All Navaho ceremonials were expensive undertakings. The singer or shaman putting on the chant had to be paid, as did his assistants. Equipment, such as deerskins, herbs, and the like, had to be purchased. And far from least, all those who attended the ceremonial had to be fed. For a nine-day chant this could be expensive.

Perhaps the most colorful part of Navaho curing ceremonies are the sand paintings or dry paintings. Sand paintings are also made by Pueblo and Apache Indians, but these are not as elaborate as those of the Navahos. According to Navaho legend, these sand paintings are sacred pictures of events in the lives of the Holy People. More than five hundred different sand paintings have so far been recorded. Each one is traditional for a particular ceremony. Several may be made as part of the treatment for an individual, the number and size of the paintings depending upon the health and wealth of the patient.

Sand paintings are generally made inside the hogan, where the curing ceremony is being held. Some paintings are small, only a foot or 2 feet in diameter; others are extremely large, up to 15 to 20 feet across. They are made under the direction of the medicine man, his assistants varying in number from one or two up to fifteen according to the size and complexity of the sand painting. For paint the Indians use dry pigments of cornmeal, pollen, charcoal, pulverized minerals, and ground-up red, yellow, and white sandstone. Although paintings are occasionally made on buckskin, most are usually made on a layer of clean sand spread on the floor of the hogan.

The shaman and his assistants dribble the varicolored vegetable and mineral pigments between thumb and forefinger, skillfully creating lightning symbols, sacred mountains, rainbows, clouds, figures of the Holy People, and corn, squash, beans, and tobacco, the four sacred plants. The pattern for this sand painting is carried in the mind of the medicine man who made it. Like the songs and rituals, these sand paintings are so complicated that it is impossible for one man to know more than a few of them. Like the songs and other rituals, the patterns and symbolism are handed down through memory from one medicine man to another.

Yet these unusual and beautiful sand paintings last for only a very few hours. They must be destroyed before sundown of the same day that they are made. When the sand painting is finished, the patient is seated on it so that he can come into direct communion with the Holy People. After certain ritual treatments, the patient leaves and the medicine man and his assistants sweep the sand painting into a deerskin or cloth, carry it outside the hogan, and ritually get rid of it.

Most Apache ceremonies were also primarily for curing. Many of them lasted for four days and, like those of the Navaho, involved songs, prayers, sacred paraphernalia, ceremonial smoking, masked dancers, and sand paintings. The use of color in an Apache ceremony followed a symbolic directional pattern—black for the east, blue for the south, yellow for the west, and white for the north.

Navaho sand painting made in a hogan for a curing ceremony.
(Tad Nichols)

If a particular ceremony failed to cure the patient, the failure could be blamed on faulty diagnosis, and another shaman might be called in to perform a different ceremony. If the patient died, the failure could be blamed on the medicine man not having been called in soon enough. Or it could be blamed on the patient's carelessness in following the shaman's taboos or even on the power of an opposing witch.

Like Navaho ceremonies, most Apache ceremonies were large or small affairs, depending on how the family was able to take care of the expense.

One of the most colorful and dramatic of all Apache ceremonials was the four-day puberty ceremony that took place when a girl came of age. One of the highlights of this coming-out ceremony was the dance put on by four masked Gan dancers representing the Mountain Spirits. A fifth masked dancer, a clown, imitated the movements of the others and served as comic relief. This dance is often mistakingly called the Devil Dance.

Like most Navaho chants and ceremonies, the Apache coming-out ceremony and other large ceremonies were also important social events. They were usually accompanied by all-night social dances, along with singing and feasting. Today Navaho Squaw Dances are so popular that white people frequently take part in them.

It is difficult to separate religion and ceremony from other phases of Navaho and Apache life. These Indians lived and breathed religion, even in warfare. The Apache man was never more conscious of religion than when he was preparing to go out and fight. Before the warriors left, there was a war dance to gain the aid of the supernatural spirits. And there was a big victory dance when they returned. One or two medicine men who had war power generally accompanied a large war party. On the journey the war shaman told them which trails to follow to ensure success. He also prayed before the attack, turning in each of the four directions. Each warrior carried a small medicine bag of sacred meal for morning and evening sacrifice. Many also carried protective charms or amulets (quartz crystals, obsidian, sandstone concretions, pieces of petrified wood, and the like), which were supposed to ward off enemy blows. Some wore special buckskin shirts painted with signs believed to protect the wearer. Others wore similar protective buckskin hats. While the war party was gone, the women, especially the wives and relatives of the warriors, had to behave carefully so that they would not give bad luck to the men.

11

Southwestern Arts and Crafts

THESE TWENTY-ODD Indian tribes of the Southwest are a colorful people. So too is their country. And their arts and crafts are equally colorful.

We call anything made by these Indians—pottery, basketry, kachina dolls, drums, moccasins, jewelry, rugs and blankets and other woven articles—their arts and crafts. To the Indian these were originally practical and necessary objects to be used every day around the home. There were few prehistoric art forms that had no real function in village or tribal life. Each was a part of the social, economic, and ceremonial activities of the particular tribe. Any artistic merit a decorated basket or pot might have had was simply considered a necessary part of good workmanship.

In other words, Southwestern Indian pots and baskets were not fine arts in the sense of today's "art for art's sake." This concept was almost unknown to the Indian.

This brings up another question. A lot has been said,

139

and much more has been written, about symbols and symbolism in Indian art. The word "symbol" has had a great appeal to buyers of Indian curios, who like to think that there is a hidden meaning behind every design on every pot and basket and ring. Some dealers in Indian crafts will even tell a colorful story to go along with an Indian-made bracelet or other object just to help make a sale.

Despite the fascination this subject seems to hold for most of us, these stories are simply products of the white man's imagination and have no basis in fact. The designs have no "meanings" as such. They are not symbols for ideas or words. The pattern used on a pottery jar does not tell a story. The figures are not symbolic. They do not have a ceremonial significance. One might as well ask the meaning of the design on the wallpaper in a modern bedroom or the pattern on a set of china.

Most ethnologists, along with most Indians, will tell you that nonreligious designs have no meaning other than the obvious one. Identifying names are often given to certain Indian designs and design elements. A triangle might be called an arrowhead or a mountain, a wavy or zigzag line a snake or lightning. A semicircle with a number of small lines projecting down from its base represents, at least to the Pueblo Indians, a rain cloud and raindrops. Naming a design, however, does not make it a symbol. The Indian potter or weaver or silversmith is thinking only of the decorative value of his work and not of any secret meaning. Even though any enterprising Indian can come up with a good explanation, there are no secret meanings to designs, except, of course, where ritualistic or ceremonial equipment is concerned.

In a Navaho sand painting made during a curing

ceremony every feature in it—pigments, colors, directions, figures—has a definite symbolic meaning. But when the same figures of Navaho divinities, or *yeis,* as they are called, are woven into a design on a Navaho blanket, they are merely decorative designs, not symbolic figures. The rug or blanket itself is never used in the ceremony and cannot be called ceremonial in any sense of the word.

Symbolism does exist on almost everything used in rituals and ceremonies. Pottery, basketry, textiles, and wooden implements and the like used in ceremonies by the Pueblos and other Southwestern Indians have painted or carved or woven designs that are symbolic. Navaho Indians, for instance, look on the bull-roarer as representing the voice of the thunderbird, whose figure they frequently paint on it. Hopi, Zuni, and Apache bull-roarers usually bear lightning symbols for the same reason.

But such sacred objects are rarely seen by non-Indians. The everyday household pottery and objects made for sale only to other Indians or to tourists are now made with little or no regard for symbolism. The decorations are merely combinations of elements which generations of craft workers have made popular in that particular pueblo or village or tribe. Actually, the only person who can explain or interpret a particular design is the one who made it. Pamphlets that claim to interpret Indian designs are not based on Indian legends or customs or beliefs. You might call them further evidence of the inventiveness of the white man's imagination.

Southwestern Indian arts and crafts are still living arts. Most of them have a long history of development. Some, like pottery and basketry and weaving and woodworking, can be traced back for over two thousand years.

Others, like silverwork and painting, are barely a century old.

The introduction of cheap and, in many ways, more serviceable metal kitchen and household implements and utensils caused many native crafts to degenerate and, in some cases, to disappear. If it had not been for non-Indian demand for native art products, most of these Indian arts and crafts probably would have long since vanished.

Basketry is probably the oldest of all Indian handicrafts in the Southwest. Some of the finest and most colorful baskets in the Southwest were those made by the Basket Maker Indians in the Four Corners country two thousand years ago. It has often been called "mother of the craft arts."

At the present time, however, basketry is on the decline in the Southwest. In most villages and tribes where lots of baskets were formerly made, basketry is either a dead or a dying art. From a strictly economic point of view this is readily understandable as few basketry weavers earn more than fifteen cents an hour for their labors. This has discouraged most of the younger Indians from learning this native industry.

Yet even today baskets are still important in both the everyday and ceremonial life of the Indians. Baskets are needed and used at one time or another during most Navaho curing ceremonies, as they are also in the marriage ceremony. Papago Indians still use watertight baskets in some of their ceremonies. Most Hopis find daily use for sifter baskets in the home. The Hopis also give coiled basketry plaques to the winners of foot races. Even in tribes where basketry is a lost art, baskets are still in demand and are eagerly sought in trade.

Only a few Indians in New Mexico make baskets now.

Navaho woman shearing sheep.

(Tad Nichols)

Some of the Pueblo Indians at Jemez make plaited baskets of yucca or bear grass, while some of the other Pueblo Indians weave wickerwork baskets of willow. The Jicarilla Apaches in northern New Mexico make a limited number of coiled baskets. To the south the Mescalero Apaches produce a few coiled bowls of split yucca. The Navahos make few baskets today, buying most of those they need for weddings and ceremonies from the Utes and Paiutes. These are woven with typical Navaho designs.

Today the Indians of Arizona produce most of the baskets made in the Southwest. And two tribes, the Hopis and Papagos, are responsible for nearly all of these.

The Hopi Indians of Second Mesa make excellent tightly woven coiled bowls and basketry plaques decorated in red, black, and yellow on the white or natural yucca-colored background. In the Third Mesa villages the Hopis make only wicker baskets, flat plaques, trays, and bowls, woven of rabbit brush or sumac colored with native-made vegetable dyes, as a rule. These baskets are also brilliantly colored in black and yellow and green and blue and white. Most of the larger and deeper wicker baskets now end up as wastebaskets. The villages on all three mesas use plaited yucca sifter baskets woven over a willow ring. In fact, the Hopis themselves are probably their own best customers for their baskets.

The Papago Indians of southern Arizona perhaps make more baskets than any other tribe in the United States. During 1963 it is estimated that Papago weavers produced more than eight thousand baskets. These basket makers ranged in age from a girl of five to a matron of eighty-seven. A typical Papago basket is built up over a foundation coil of bear grass sewn with strips of bleached yucca and the black outer covering of the devil's-claw seedpod. To add a variety of colors, the weavers also used the natural green and yellow of yucca, and red from the roots of the narrow leaf yucca, along with desert willow. Designs are simple geometric patterns or figures of humans and animals. The Papagos also make hundreds of soft-weave baskets of yucca, turned out primarily for sale to tourists.

The Pimas, who used to make many finely woven baskets, now make very few. One authority doubts that more than fifty baskets a year are now being woven by Pima women.

The Western Apaches, once famous for their finely woven and decorated basketry, now make few baskets. They still make an occasional wicker burden or carrying basket decorated with three or four horizontal colored bands encircling the basket and a number of dangling buckskin fringes. The Western Apaches also make water jars or canteens. These are tall, narrow-necked baskets with the inside, and frequently the outside as well, coated with melted pinyon pitch to make them watertight. To prevent the water from spilling out, the top is plugged with a wad of clean grass or juniper bark.

Most of the other tribes in Arizona—the Havasupais, Walapais, Yavapais, Paiutes, Maricopas, and Chemehuevis—still make baskets, but only in very limited numbers.

Like basketry, weaving is another extremely ancient art in the Southwest. The Basket Makers were weaving sandals out of yucca cord in the early centuries of the Christian Era. They were also weaving flexible bags of Indian hemp string decorated with woven or painted designs in black and red on the natural yellow-brown background. The Basket Makers even made blankets

Even small girls learn how to card yarn.

(Tad Nichols)

out of yucca wound with fur or feather cord. Most of the Pueblo Indians wove cotton textiles as early as A.D. 700 or 750. The oldest known piece of cotton fabric is believed to have been made about A.D. 858. Down in southern Arizona the Hohokam peoples were probably weaving cotton into cloth long before that.

146

The Pueblo Indians seem to have reached the peak of their development in weaving during the thirteenth and fourteenth centuries. Although plain and tapestry weaves were the most common, there were also such fancy weaves as gauze, brocading, and embroidery. The Indians made large and small blankets, aprons, sashes, breechcloths, headbands, kilts, and leggings. Men were the weavers then as now. The introduction of sheep from Mexico by the Spaniards in the sixteenth century added a new textile material—wool. The Pueblo Indians continued to weave their ceremonial wearing apparel and other paraphernalia in native cotton but began to use wool for items of everyday wear.

Native cotton yarn was a creamy white color, while wool might be either white or black or various shades of gray or brown. Both cotton and wool could be dyed with native plants (vegetable dyes) to give yellow, black, red, orange, and green. Native cotton, as well as wool, was cleaned and straightened by hand and was also spun by hand with a spindle stick and attached spindle whorl. The coming of Anglo-Americans in the middle and latter part of the nineteenth century brought in Germantown and other commercial wool yarns, along with aniline dyes and commercial cotton.

At the present time the Hopis are, with a few exceptions, the only Pueblo Indians still carrying on this ancient tradition. A Hopi man sets up his loom in his house or, as in the old days, in a kiva. Evidences of looms and loom weights have been found in kivas in a great many ancient Pueblo Indian ruins. In former times, and up until recent years, Hopi men raised the cotton which they used. Now they buy balls of string at the nearest trading post.

Tradition is still strong in this craft. Although most

147

Hopis and other Pueblos have shifted to European clothing and commercial cloth for everyday wear, native woven materials, usually of cotton, are still preferred for ceremonial use. That is why you can still find a few Hopi men weaving ceremonial kilts and sashes and blankets for their own use and for trade with the other Pueblo peoples who no longer weave. Some Hopis are also making vegetable dye wool rugs and other articles for sale to tourists.

Up until the late nineteenth century, Pimas and Papagos were raising and weaving cotton into cradle bands and blankets. Now what cotton they raise is for the commercial market. And they do no weaving at all. Formerly the Colorado River and plateau Yumans, along with the Paiutes, made rabbit-skin blankets.

Today Southwestern weaving is largely in the hands of its most recent Indian arrivals, the Navahos. These are the most famous of all Southwestern weavers. Here, however, the woman, not the man, is the weaver. The Navahos probably learned the art from the Pueblo Indians in the late seventeenth and early eighteenth centuries, when many Pueblo Indians sought refuge with the Navahos after the Pueblo Rebellion of 1680. As proof of this, all of the basic Navaho processes, from spinning with shaft and spindle whorl to weaving on a simple portable upright loom, were identical with Pueblo techniques. Traditional Navaho clothing also closely resembled Pueblo attire—striped shoulder blanket and the Navaho woman's blanket dress and the man's shirt.

During the 1700's, with sheep obtained from the Spanish, either by trade or by theft, and the technique of weaving learned from the Pueblo Indians, the Navahos became widely known as weavers. By 1800, if not before, they had surpassed their Pueblo teachers and were sup-

Navaho woman weaving a rug.

(Tad Nichols)

plying native woven textiles to other Indians and to Spaniards as well.

We have, unfortunately, few actual examples of Navaho weaving prior to 1850. The oldest fragments were found in Massacre Cave in Cañon del Muerto (Canyon of the Dead) in northeastern Arizona, where a group of Navaho women and children were killed in 1805 by Spanish soldiers.

The golden or classic age of Navaho weaving came during the period from about 1850 to 1875. Throughout this time Navaho women were weaving articles of clothing for their own families and blankets both for themselves and for sale or trade to other Indians, Mexicans, and Americans.

After the return of the Navahos to their home country in 1868 from Fort Sumner, New Mexico, changes in weaving took place. These resulted from the introduction of commercial yarns and dyes and commercial clothing and yard goods. After 1890, increasing tourist trade brought a demand for rugs rather than blankets. With these heavier floor coverings came changes in color and style of designs. During this dark age in Navaho weaving, from 1890 to about 1920, quality declined and native designs almost disappeared. Then came a change for the better, largely owing to the efforts of traders and other individuals and groups interested in raising the standard of Navaho weaving. There was a revival of old blanket patterns and a return to the native vegetable dyes, which produced much softer and quieter colors than the aniline dyes. Today some eighty different dye recipes, using a wide variety of native plants and berries and fruit and flowers, have been developed.

Although the quality of Navaho weaving is relatively high today, the quantity is declining year by year. You can see why when you learn that a 3-foot by 5-foot rug of average quality requires some three hundred and fifty hours of work. No Navaho weaver can earn a living at that rate, even at today's high prices. And spinning, dyeing, and weaving are not easy jobs. Under these conditions, most authorities doubt that the craft can survive much longer.

The art of pottery making in the Southwest is not as old as that of either basketry or weaving. But it still goes back, at least in southern Arizona and New Mexico, a little more than two thousand years, a respectable antiquity. From there, centuries later, it spread northward to the Pueblo Indians.

Although no two pots ever looked exactly alike, certain vessel shapes and colors and styles of design and methods of manufacture were the fashion in each village or regional or tribal area. But like the fads and fashions of today, change was the rule. Every fifty or a hundred years or so the potters scrapped the old styles and developed new forms and patterns of decoration. Using a chronology based on these variations, archaeologists can tell at a glance where and approximately when a prehistoric pot was made.

This is equally true of modern pottery. Clay pots and pans are still being made by most of the Pueblo Indians and by some of the other Indians in the Southwest. Color and design patterns are traditional and, in general, each pueblo and each tribe stick closely to their own—like the black and yellow colors and conventionalized bird patterns of the Hopi, the deer designs and owl effigies of the Zuni, the floral designs of Zia Pueblo, the highly polished red and black pottery of San Ildefonso and Santa Clara, the geometric designs of Santo Domingo, the cylindrical pots with pointed bottoms so characteristic of the Navaho.

At present these Indians make comparatively little

pottery for their own use. Commercially manufactured dishes and pots and pans are too easily available. Most pottery produced now is geared to the tourist trade.

This is, however, made in the same way as prehistoric pottery. It is authentic Indian pottery, made by Indian women who learned the art from their mothers or grandmothers. Indian women dig up the clay from local deposits, grind it up, and mix it with a tempering material such as sand or pulverized rock or potsherds. They build up the walls of their pots by coiling long ropes or rolls of clay into the desired shape. It is entirely handmade, none of the American Indians ever having used the potter's wheel. After the vessel has been built up by the successive coils of clay, the walls are scraped and smoothed with a piece of dried gourd. When the pot has dried for a time, a slip, a mixture of fine clay and water, is wiped on to form a smooth surface. This is usually given a final polish with a smooth, water-worn pebble. If a design is planned, it is painted on with brushes made from the chewed ends of yucca leaves. Papagos use the tip of the devil's-claw bush for a paintbrush.

As in former days, paints are made from the juices of such plants as beeweed and tansy mustard or from iron and manganese and other minerals. Finally, the pots have to be fired to harden the clay. Wood was the usual fuel until the introduction of domestic animals, and broken pieces of pottery were used to protect the pots from the burning wood. Now cow or sheep dung is often used for fuel, and sheets of scrap iron form the firing oven.

Only a few of the other Southwestern Indian tribes are still making pottery. The Southern Paiutes and Western Apaches used to make pots like the pointed-bottom ones that the Navahos made. But they haven't

Navaho silversmith and the tools of his trade.
(Tad Nichols)

made pottery for a number of years. The Yavapai and Walapai and Havasupai made little pottery in the past and make none today. Their downriver Yuman-speaking relatives, the Mohave and Yuma and Cocopa, all of whom used to make quite a lot of red-on-buff and plain buff-colored pottery, make little or no pottery today. In fact, there is said to be only one surviving Mohave potter.

Of the three tribes in southern and central Arizona—the Pima and Papago and Maricopa—none of them

153

make pottery in the quantities that they formerly did. Only the Papagos make very much pottery, and most of this is for the tourist trade. For their own use they make bowls and jars or ollas and bean pots. For sale to tourists they make ashtrays, flower vases, dishes, and other similar pieces, often decorating them with simple geometric patterns in black on the polished red background.

Navaho Indian silversmiths are famous the world over, and Navaho jewelry has found its way to almost every country on earth. Because it is so widely known, Indian silverwork is usually thought of as another one of the ancient arts.

Yet actually it is one of the most recent. And it is an adopted art at that, the Navahos having learned to work with silver from Mexican silversmiths about the middle of the nineteenth century. They soon excelled their teachers, and their handmade products in silver are now their proudest possession.

At first the Indians used silver quarters and dollars. When such use was finally prohibited by United States law in 1890, the Navaho smiths began using Mexican pesos, which were richer in silver content and easier to work. In 1930, however, Mexico put a stop to the export of its silver coins. Today the Indian smiths use sterling silver in bar, sheet, or wire form. They never did mine their own silver.

The objects they make, both for their own use and for the tourist trade, are largely items for personal wear—finger rings, buttons, bracelets, earrings, conchas (*concha* is the Spanish word for shell) for belts, necklaces, hatbands, belt buckles, pins, tie clasps, cuff links, and the like.

The so-called squash-blossom necklace is one of the most common types of Navaho jewelry. It consists of hollow silver beads separated by long, flower-shaped pendants, with a larger crescent-shaped ornament dangling at the front of the necklace. Actually, the squash blossom should be called a pomegranate, since it is an elongated version of the small silver pomegranate formerly used to decorate Mexican trousers and jackets. The terminal crescent, or *naja,* probably came from the Old World by way of Spain, where the Spaniards adopted it from the Moors of North Africa.

The first Navaho silversmithing, made with the crudest of homemade tools, was hammered work, decorated with only simple incised or stamped designs. Not until about 1880 did the Indians begin to use settings in their silver jewelry. Bits of glass, native garnet, buttons, beads, and jet were first tried but were never very popular.

But once turquoise began to be used for settings, it quickly surpassed all others. This hard, deep blue to green stone has been highly prized by Southwestern Indians since Basket Maker days. In prehistoric times the Indians mined turquoise with stone picks and hammers, some mines extending several hundred feet underground. Turquoise was one of the most popular of all trade items. Although turquoise was used primarily to make beads and pendants and necklaces and other ornaments, it was also highly favored as an offering in important ceremonies.

About 1870 some of the Pueblo Indians also went into the silversmithing business. Their ancestors had been fashioning turquoise and shell and bone and other materials into ornaments for hundreds of years. So it was easy for them to make the switch to silver. Of all the Pueblos, the Indians of Zuni rank practically on a par with the Navahos in the production of jewelry. In fact, many Navahos wear silver jewelry made by the Zuni

Indians. As a general rule, the Zunis emphasize the turquoise in their silverwork, using more turquoise and cut shell and less silver, while the Navahos use more silver and less turquoise.

To many Southwestern Indians, turquoise and silver jewelry are more treasured than money. Many Indian women, especially Navahos, keep all their wealth on their arms and necks, not in the bank. Often Navahos will convert their cash into silver and turquoise jewelry. Later, when they need money or credit, they will use a bracelet or a belt as security for a loan from the trading post. In trading post vaults, where such "pawn" is held until it is redeemed, you can see some of the finest Navaho and Pueblo turquoise and silverwork.

Still another phase of Southwestern Indian art can be seen in the carved wooden figures of kachinas or masked dancers. In Chapter 6 we mentioned that the kachinas, particularly to the Hopis and Zunis, represented the spirits of departed ancestors and other supernatural beings who served as go-betweens for humans and the more important gods. While the Indian belief in kachinas is ancient, the making of kachina dolls is probably not more than a century or two old.

These dolls are made by the men and given to the children as gifts during the kachina ceremonies. They are not idols and are not worshiped but are used in the religious education of the youngsters to teach them the names and characteristics of the more than two hundred different kachinas.

Today kachina dolls are also made for sale. Hopis carve them from chunks of the root of dead cottonwood trees, while Zuni men generally use pine wood. Yet even those dolls made for sale are elaborately carved and painted and are faithful representations of definite

Hopi kachina dolls.
(Arizona State Museum)

kachinas. Each has a name—sun, wolf, eagle, owl, mud-head, black ogre, spotted corn—and each has a mask and clothing carved and painted in the likeness of the kachina it portrays. Protruding horns, ears, noses, and headdresses are carefully fitted on with tiny wooden pegs. Many are further embellished with small colorful feathers and carry rattles or bows and arrows or other objects in their hands.

In recent years some Navahos have begun carving

wooden dolls representing the *yeis,* the intermediaries between men and gods, each complete with carved and painted costume and mask and other ritual paraphernalia.

Bead-making is another ancient craft of the Southwestern Indians. Every Indian tribe made beads of shell or stone or turquoise or bone or some other material.

Seashell, perhaps the most common bead-making material, has been an important trade item in the Southwest for nearly two thousand years. Clam, conus, olivella, abalone, and other shells from the Pacific coast or the Gulf of California were carried to the inland peoples by early Indian traders.

Making circular bone beads was easy, merely calling for the cutting of sections from the thigh or other hollow long bones of birds and animals. But making disk-shaped beads of shell, stone, and turquoise required a lot more effort. The shell or stone had to be broken or cut up into irregularly shaped pieces somewhat larger than the finished bead. Each piece then had to be drilled through the middle. Finally, the fragments were strung on a cord and rolled back and forth on a fine-grained sandstone slab until they became smooth and round. Today a few bead-makers at Zuni and Santo Domingo pueblos manufacture most of the shell beads used in the Southwest.

Coral beads, imported from Italy and introduced into the Southwest by the Spaniards, have replaced the reddish stone beads formerly made by the Indians. These rounded or tubular beads are now favorite ornaments. It is said that Navahos will spend a lot of time and effort trying to match strands of coral.

Colored glass beads were more recent arrivals in the Southwest. They were quickly adopted by the Apaches,

Navaho artist, Harrison Begay, and some of his Indian paintings.
(Tad Nichols)

Utes, and Yuman tribes. The Apaches sewed them on their buckskin shirts and jackets as decoration. Later they wove them into headbands and belts and necklaces for sale. So did some of the Yuman tribes.

Painting on paper is the newest medium to be taken

up by Southwestern Indians. Painting itself, of course, was already an ancient art when the first Spanish explorers came up from Mexico. For nearly two thousand years aboriginal artists had been decorating pottery, stone, bone, textiles, the rock walls of caves, and the plastered walls of ceremonial chambers with brush and paint. Archaeologists have excavated several prehistoric kivas in northern Arizona and New Mexico where the plastered walls had been covered with beautiful murals. At the ancient pueblo of Kuaua, New Mexico, now the Coronado State Monument, the kiva walls were coated with at least eighty-five thin layers of clay plaster, seventeen of which were decorated with paintings.

Today descendants of these long vanished artists use paper and commercial colors to re-create ancient tribal customs and religious symbols and to portray Indian country and its everyday life.

Southwestern Indian painting on paper began in the early years of the twentieth century. But it didn't really get going until 1932, when the Bureau of Indian Affairs established a painting class in the Santa Fe Indian School. Young Hopis and Zunis and Indians from most of the other pueblos flocked to the class, along with Navahos and Jicarilla Apaches and Western Apaches.

Modern Indian painting is distinctive, entirely original, uniquely American. It is highly decorative and imaginative, usually two-dimensional, and done in a flat, opaque watercolor technique. The Indian painter uses no models, working entirely from memory. He follows no color theory. Often the background is left to the imagination.

Many of these Indian artists are producing fine work —Navahos Harrison Begay and Beatien Yazz, the Apache Allan Houser, Pablita Velarde of Santa Clara, Gilbert Atencio of San Ildefonso, Velino Herrera of Zia, the Jicarilla Apache Sylvia Vicenti, and Hopi artists Gibson Talahytewa and Roderick Holmes, to name only a few.

Baskets, textiles, silverwork, pottery, kachina dolls, and paintings aren't the only craft items made by Southwestern Indians. Formerly, of course, the Indians had to provide themselves with all their own tools, implements, utensils, weapons, and ceremonial paraphernalia. Many of these have disappeared entirely during these days of ready access to manufactured goods. But others still linger on.

Bows and arrows are rarely used in hunting today. A few are still used for certain ceremonies. But many more are manufactured to sell to tourists.

Navahos and Apaches and Hopis, along with some other Indians, still make and wear moccasins. Buckskin is still used for the upper part of most moccasins, while cowhide has largely supplanted elkhide for the sole. Most Indians still sew moccasins together with sinew.

Drums and rattles and flutes were the principal musical instruments of most Southwestern Indians, and they are still being made for use in ceremonies. Pueblo Indians made their drums out of hollowed sections of cottonwood trees, covering the ends with goat or horsehide. Navahos simply covered the open end of a pot with skin. Most Indians made rattles out of gourds and flutes out of cane.

Most prehistoric Southwestern Indians used fetishes or charms, like our rabbit's foot, which were thought to have magic power. Today the Zunis make most of the fetishes used in the Southwest. The ones usually seen on sale are hunting fetishes, carved from shell, stone, or antler in the form of lions and eagles and bears and other animals. Sometimes turquoise or shell beads or

161

small feathers are tied to the animals to increase their power.

Baby cradles or carriers are still made and used by Navahos and Apaches and Hopis. Most of them also make cloth or buckskin dolls for sale.

These Southwestern Indians are inventive and highly imaginative. Each year their productive minds seem to come up with something new or something modified from the past in the way of arts and crafts.

12

Southwestern Indians in the Modern World

Lo, THE POOR INDIAN is not vanishing, at least
not in the Southwest. According to estimates made by
archaeologists, the Southwest probably had about
103,000 Indians living there when the first Europeans
arrived on the scene in 1539–40. Today there are over
150,000. There are more Indians in the Southwest than
there are in any other section of the United States.

The largest single Indian tribe in the United States
and Canada is the Navaho, with a population of slightly
more than 100,000. They live on the largest Indian reservation in the United States, a vast domain of 25,000
square miles in northeastern Arizona and northwestern
New Mexico, whose broad acres are even bigger than
some states.

In no other part of the country are there as many
Indians who continue to speak their own languages and
follow their own social and religious customs. Nowhere
in the United States does a visitor get the feeling of an-

tiquity that he does in the Southwest. There you can see Indians living almost exactly the same kinds of lives as did their ancestors of five hundred to a thousand years ago.

Another unique feature about the Southwest is that nearly every one of its twenty-odd different Indian tribes is still living in practically the same area where their ancestors once roamed. The only major exception is the Chiricahua Apache tribe. After Geronimo's surrender in 1886, the last of the Chiricahuas, 502 in all, were shipped off to prison in Florida. From there they were transferred to Alabama, and in 1894 the 407 survivors were sent to Fort Sill, Oklahoma. In 1913, 187 Chiricahuas were allowed to join their cousins on the Mescalero Reservation in southern New Mexico. The rest elected to remain in Oklahoma, where their descendants still live.

Yet even though the rest of the Southwest's Indians still live in or next to their ancestral homelands, in most cases that homeland is greatly reduced from what it was at the time of the Spanish discovery. The Yavapais, who used to range from the Colorado to the Verde, are now confined to three small reservations in central Arizona. Nor does the vast Papago Indian Reservation, second only to the Navaho in size, stretching for 60 miles along the Arizona-Mexican border and reaching northward for nearly 100 miles, cover anywhere near the territory over which these Indians formerly made their living.

Archaeological evidence confirms this, pointing to a much wider area of occupation for every tribe as compared with present-day boundaries of reservations.

In addition to losing lands, some tribes have been shoved into the least desirable portions of their former territory. This has backfired, however, in at least one instance. The Four Corners country was thought to be good for nothing, fit only for Indians. Yet this land of the Navahos, a land of painted deserts and mesas and canyons, rocky and sandy and dry, has made the Navaho tribe rich as a result of oil and uranium and gas leases. The Navahos cleared over $1,000,000 during 1967 on Arizona oil royalties alone. And not too long ago coal was discovered on the reservation, a deposit containing over half a billion tons. This has already brought in a huge, multi-million-dollar steam generating plant. Powered by the coal, this plant will furnish electricity to the Navahos for industrial as well as domestic purposes.

Experts have been predicting for the past century that all the old Indian ways would disappear with the next generation. But that next generation never seems to arrive.

Some Indians have managed to achieve a happy balance between their own culture and that of the white man. Others have been badly bent, but not quite broken, under the burden of the meeting of such greatly different civilizations. Some Indian groups have preserved parts of the old and accepted what they wished of the new. Despite the new and radically altered way of life, some tribes have increased tremendously in numbers, like the Navahos and Apaches and many of the Pueblos. Others have dwindled under disease and other pressures from outside. There are, for example, fewer than a hundred Cocopas still living in Arizona. But none of these tribes has been completely decimated.

In this balancing of cultures the Southwestern Indian has retained certain portions of his organization, particularly in religion, and certain of his craft arts. On the other hand, he has accepted from the white man education and health facilities and political organization.

Indian programs, both the official ones of the Bureau

of Indian Affairs and the unofficial, have in recent years been concentrated upon the introduction of modern sanitation and health practices, the education of Indian children, and the raising of living standards through the introduction of American economic practices and the development of reservation resources.

Most Indians of today recognize, at least in theory, the value of education, modern medicine, and the American economic system. Practice of these, however, varies considerably from pueblo to pueblo or from tribe to tribe.

Where native curing was on an individual basis, it has tended to die out. Where healing functioned at the community level, and as a religious ceremony, it has persisted.

In the matter of education, our American school system has been difficult for the Indians to accept. It is completely foreign to their way of life. At first, practically all Southwestern Indian groups opposed the government's educational efforts. They did not want their children taken away to Indian boarding schools. And they opposed the building of Indian day schools to take care of the younger children in their home communities on the reservation.

Many Indians claimed that schooling interfered with their economic and religious pursuits. Navahos, for example, opposed schools of any kind because they took the children away from herding sheep.

Of all Southwestern tribes the Navahos have most consistently taxed the ingenuity of the Bureau of Indian Affairs in its attempts to provide school facilities. The Navaho reservation is huge; its Indian population is greater than that of all other Southwestern tribes combined. More important, Navahos are not clustered in pueblos or villages, as most of the other Indians are, but live in scattered family groups, moving with their flocks of sheep between summer and winter homes.

Not too many years ago less than half the children in some of the larger pueblos were permitted by their parents to attend the day schools.

Today this has changed. There are good schools on every reservation. Most young Indians now attend regular public schools. Indian children are even allowed to go back home from the Pueblo Indian boarding schools so that they can take part in religious dances and ceremonies. Most Indian children have the opportunity to finish at least the eighth grade. More and more Indians, however, are realizing the benefits of higher education. They know that, in most cases, there is neither enough land nor enough opportunity for all the people to make a living at home.

To prepare their children for work in the outside world, the Navahos have set up a $10,000,000 trust fund, the income to provide future scholarships, particularly for young men and women who wish to train for professions.

Even though all of the younger and most of the middle-aged Indians in the villages and pueblos speak English, you might still call it a second language. The language of the Navaho reservation, for instance, is Navaho. The same is true for every other Indian reservation in the Southwest. Native languages are still very much alive.

To most Southwestern Indians, the concept of the white man's democratic form of government was strange. Forming a tribal government of any sort wasn't easy for peoples who had never before been organized on a tribal basis. Tribal unity seldom existed, something it often took military authorities, who thought they were dealing with *the* chief, too long to learn. In prereservation days no one chief ever spoke for all of the Navahos. Nor did any one Chiricahua or Western Apache chief ever speak for all of the Chiricahuas or Western Apaches. Treaties made with one local headman were ignored by the others.

But the Indian Reorganization Act of 1934 brought this condition to an end. Important features of this act were the provisions for Indian self-government and enterprises, permitting Indians to elect officers, manage their local affairs, own land as a corporation, and borrow money from the government for farm improvements and advanced scholarships. Nearly all Southwestern Indians have organized their villages or tribe under this act and now have democratically elected tribal councils.

Oddly enough, the tribal council concept of democratic government has had its biggest success in those tribes which never thought of themselves as tribes. The Navahos now have a tribal council, with elections being held every four years. Campaigning before elections is active. Voters, both men and women over twenty-one must register to vote. Voting is done by ballot on which the candidates' photographs, as well as names, are printed for the benefit of the illiterate. Women can and do serve on the council. Both the San Carlos and White Mountain groups of the Western Apaches also have elected tribal councils. Like the Navahos, the Apaches are keenly interested in council affairs. Voting for council members is generally heavy.

Tribal government didn't come so easily to the Hopis. Each Hopi village is like a separate independent state, with its own government and its own origin and history. For years some of the larger villages refused to vote in tribal elections and refused to concede that the tribal council represented them.

One of the hardest things for the Indians to accept was the American economic system. Its private property concepts, capital investments and business, thrift, savings, and the like made little sense to most Indians. By now, however, most tribes have learned to accept at least certain features of the system.

Indian economy has changed. Hunting and gathering are of relatively little importance today in most tribes. Papagos, however, still gather giant cactus fruit and other desert plants. So do many Apaches. Most tribes are now farmers, and small farm plots have become bigger ones. Spades and hoes and plows, as well as tractors and other mechanical farm equipment, have replaced the ancient digging stick and carrying basket.

For its size the Mohave Indian reservation along the Colorado River is one of the wealthier reservations. Its Mohave and Chemehuevi residents have become large-scale farmers, raising such cash crops as cotton and alfalfa. Little of Mohave aboriginal culture survives today. Yet conservative Mohaves still practice cremation in the old style.

Herding, formerly unknown in the Southwest, is now common. The Western Apaches have become fine cattlemen, while the Navahos own thousands of flocks of sheep. The Western Apaches have gone into the cattle business in a big way. Along with a number of cattle associations for individual Apaches, both the San Carlos and White Mountain Apaches have their own tribal herds of fine Hereford cattle. Many Papagos and Utes and Mohaves and Pueblos have also become cattlemen. In addition to sheep, Navahos have thousands of horses and cattle and goats.

Many Southwestern Indians have also become wage earners, working as mechanics, machine operators,

Irrigating a field on the Mohave Indian Reservation on the Colorado River.

(Tad Nichols)

clerks, and laborers off their reservations. This was due in part to the wholesale displacement of individuals and families during the Second World War. Indians from every Indian tribe in the Southwest were in all branches of the armed forces. Thousands of other Indians, many taking their families with them, left the reservation and took full- or part-time jobs in war industries and in agriculture. A second factor was that the building and improvement of reservation roads during the past twenty years have ended the geographical isolation of such tribes

170

as the Navahos, Apaches, Hopis, and Papagos. Indians who did not leave the reservation from one year to the next now regularly visit neighboring communities. Of the eleven thousand or more Papagos, at least half live and work in communities and areas adjacent to their reservation, many more or less permanently.

Other Indians have gone into business for themselves. Pueblo Indians have opened stores, garages, silversmith shops, and craft shops in their villages. There are even licensed Pueblo plumbers and electricians, as well as tailors and teachers and trained nurses and secretaries.

Most Southwestern tribes have also started tribal business enterprises. The White Mountain Apaches built a modern $2,000,000 sawmill employing over a hundred Indians. So did the Navahos. New electronics plants are in operation or planned on both the Papago and Navaho reservations.

In recent years many Southwestern Indians have begun to encourage tourists to visit their once-remote and secluded reservations. The Navahos and Western Apaches and Mescalero Apaches are particularly active in this field.

The Navahos, through their tribal council, have built motels and restaurants and tourist information centers and have organized a staff of Navaho rangers to serve visitors. They own several trading posts on the reservation and manage the Navaho Arts and Crafts Guild. Recognizing the importance of one of their major assets, their magnificent and often spectacular scenery, the Navahos have set aside as tribal parks half a dozen scenic and recreational areas throughout the reservation. Maintained by the Department of Parks and Recreation of the Navaho tribe, each is complete with a visitor information center, camping grounds, and picnic sites.

Indian rodeo and fairgrounds at Whiteriver, Arizona, on the White Mountain Apache Indian Reservation.

(Tad Nichols)

In 1961 the Navahos established the Navaho Tribal Museum at Window Rock, Arizona, to preserve the cultural heritage of the Navahos and of other prehistoric and historic Southwestern Indian tribes in that area. It contains outstanding displays of Navaho blankets, silver and turquoise jewelry, and other crafts. The museum's exhibits also illustrate the geology, paleontology, fauna, and flora of the region.

Window Rock, Arizona, not far from the New Mexican border, is also well worth visiting. This famous landmark, named for a giant window formed by an even bigger stone arch, now marks the capital or headquarters of the Navaho tribal government. The Navaho Tribal Council House is octagonal in shape, built like an extra large hogan.

In 1960 the Navahos began publishing their own newspaper, *The Navaho Times,* as a project of their Public Relations and Information Department. Published at Window Rock, this weekly newspaper contains a lot of information about the history and arts and crafts of the Navahos and places to visit on the reservation.

The Western Apaches have also gone into the recreation business. A few years ago the White Mountain Apaches organized the White Mountain Recreation Enterprise. They have already built cottages and motels around numerous lakes and streams on the reservation, developed hundreds of new campgrounds, improved roads and trails, and leased nearly a thousand cabin sites. Each year they plant hundreds of thousands of trout in these lakes and streams. Through the sale of fishing, camping, and hunting permits, they have added thousands of dollars to tribal revenues. The San Carlos Apaches are developing the heavily forested northern part of their reservation as a recreation area. The San

173

Carlos Indian Tribe has also just taken over the operation of recreation at San Carlos Reservoir and are planning a new boat dock, café, campground, and other facilities.

One of the Jicarilla Apache tribal enterprises centers on Dulce Lake, where the Indians have built a motel and other facilities for tourists.

Like the other Apaches, the Mescaleros have also gone into the tourist business. They have opened a tourist center on the main highway through the reservation and are encouraging the manufacture of native arts and crafts.

The San Carlos Apaches are the first tribe in the Southwest, if not in the nation, to hold membership in a chamber of commerce. On September 24, 1952, this Apache tribe joined the Safford, Arizona, Chamber of Commerce.

The homes of many of the Southwestern Indian tribes have changed. Flimsy, temporary camp structures of poles and brush have almost disappeared. Most now live in relatively permanent houses. New materials, such as brick and cement blocks, have been adopted. Wooden doors, glass windows, screens, and chimneys have been added. But the greatest change has been in furniture. Where most Indian houses formerly had only a fire pit, a few storage niches, and woven mats or rabbit-skin blankets for beds, with mealing bins and perhaps a raised bench in Pueblo houses, now they have beds, tables, chairs, lamps, stoves, sewing machines, radios, television sets, refrigerators, and washing machines.

For nearly all of the pueblo villages, along with Pimas and Papagos and Apaches and Navahos, now have electricity. It has even reached the Hopis. Many pueblos also have sewer systems, along with running water in every house.

Dress has also changed since 1540. The breechcloth, which used to be the chief, and almost the only, item of the well-dressed Indian man's attire, has survived only for ceremonial wear. Western or cowboy garb, from broad-brimmed hats to high-heeled boots, is common today. For the women, European-inspired skirts and blouses or modern American-made dresses have replaced buckskin and fiber aprons and skirts.

Arts and crafts have probably suffered the most under the impact of modern civilization. Manufactured household utensils brought an end to native basketry and pottery, except for those few tribes that make pots and baskets for white trade. Weaving has also declined. It is far easier to buy ready-made dresses or cloth in a store than it is to weave garments for the entire family. Navaho weaving has survived only because of the outside market for their colorful blankets. The Navahos themselves, and many other Indians, usually wear machine-made, Indian-style blankets manufactured in Pendleton, Oregon. Hopi weaving has hung on only because of the strength of their religious tradition.

Some form of Christianity has, outwardly at least, replaced native Indian belief in many of the Southwestern tribes. Yet most of the Hopis and Navahos and Apaches still cling to their traditional religion. So do many of the other Pueblo Indians.

It still isn't easy to get in and out of Havasu Canyon in northern Arizona, where the one hundred and eighty-six Havasupai Indians live. Mules or horses are still needed to get down the trail into the 1,000-foot-deep canyon. Autos can't get down this 14-mile trail winding along the steep canyon walls. The Havasupais live in what is perhaps the most isolated Indian village in the United States. But the Havasupais now have electric lights, hot and cold running water, refrigerators, telephones, radios,

Navaho woman frying bread dough over an open fire.
(Tad Nichols)

and even a radio transmitter. They get their mail twice a week. No longer do they move out of the valley in the fall, after the harvest, to gather seeds and hunt rabbits and deer and antelope during the winter months. Now most of them stay the year around in their village at the bottom of the canyon.

176

Pickup trucks have replaced the foot and the horse as the favorite means of transportation. Even Indian women drive heavy trucks with ease.

Yet the old way of life still goes on. Southwestern Indians may change the unimportant things, like clothing and furniture and houses and ways to make a living, but their age-old social and ceremonial customs haven't changed very much. Kivas can still be found in most pueblos, and they are still being used.

The traditional hogan—one round room of logs and mud, with a smoke hole in the roof—still is home for a great many Navaho Indians. Among the Apaches, neat frame houses have replaced pole and brush wickiups of nomadic days. But many of the latter can still be seen.

Zuni and Taos are still the skyscrapers of the Pueblo Indian world, towering five stories into the air. Except for the addition of doors and windows and chimneys, most pueblos haven't changed much outwardly over the past few centuries. There aren't as many pueblos as there were in 1540, but there are a lot more Pueblo Indians.

Most Pueblo women still grind corn by hand on ancient stone metates. Many of them, along with many Navahos and Apaches, prefer to cook over an open fire.

A picturesque feature of most pueblos, as well as of many Papago and Pima Indian villages, is the huge, dome-shaped clay oven. In spite of its looks, however, this beehive-shaped oven is not Indian. It was adopted from the Spaniards during early historic times.

Many Indians still get married in the traditional, tribal way, and marriages are often arranged by the two families rather than by the individuals themselves. Today, however, the couple also needs a marriage license and legal marriage according to the laws of that

177

particular state. And although divorce may be by old-time methods and just as easy, the government requires that the separation be legalized in court.

Although Southwestern Indian reservations during the late nineteenth century may have resembled concentration camps, they do not today. Indians are citizens of the United States and of the states in which they live. They are free to come and go as they please. Like other American citizens, they have to pay sales taxes and gasoline taxes and personal property taxes and income taxes. Like other Americans, Indians must earn their own living.

Change has come to Southwestern Indians, as it has to the rest of the world. And more change is on the way. But we hope that the Navahos and Apaches and Hopis and other Indians of the Southwest never entirely lose the essence of their native culture.

Glossary

Anasazi—Navaho Indian word meaning "the Ancient Ones," the prehistoric Basket Maker and Pueblo Indians of the Southwest.

Anthropology—The study of man and his culture.

Archaeology—The scientific study of the material remains of ancient peoples.

Artifact—Archaeological term for anything made by man.

Atlatl—Aztec Indian word for the spear-thrower used by many prehistoric peoples to hurl spears or darts.

Awl—A pointed tool, usually of bone, used to pierce hides or other materials.

Basket Maker—Prehistoric group of Indians who lived nearly two thousand years ago in the Four Corners country.

Carbon 14 or radiocarbon dating—A method of determining the age of archaeological objects of organic material by measuring the amount of disintegration of the carbon-14 atoms.

Clan—A social unit based on kinship which is reckoned on descent through one parent only.

Cliff Dwellers—Prehistoric Pueblo Indians who lived in stone houses built in caves in the cliffs.

Culture—To anthropologists, the implements and utensils and customs showing how a people lived.

Dendrochronology—A method of dating prehistoric ruins by means of the annual rings in certain trees.

Flint—A variety of quartz, such as chert or chalcedony or jasper, used by many Indians for their chipped-stone implements.

Geochronology—A combination of Greek words which means the study of time measurements of the earth, including, among others, tree ring dating and carbon 14, or radiocarbon, dating.

Hogan—The term used for the particular style of house built by the Navaho Indians.

Hohokam—A Pima Indian word for the prehistoric Indians who used to live in southern Arizona.

Kachinas—Masked impersonations of supernatural beings in Pueblo Indian religion and also used for the wooden representations made by Hopi Indians.

Kinship—The classification of relatives.

Kiva—The ceremonial chamber of the Pueblo Indians.

Mano—A hand stone used for grinding corn on a metate.

Matrilineal—Descent traced through the female line.

Matrilocal residence—A husband's residence in the house or village of his wife's kin.

Metate—The stone slab on which corn was ground.

Mogollon—An extremely early farming and pottery-making culture in eastern Arizona and western New Mexico.

Obsidian—A variety of volcanic glass used by many Indians for arrowheads and other chipped implements.

Patayan—A prehistoric culture along the lower Colorado River in western Arizona and eastern California.

Patrilineal—Descent traced through the male line.

Patrilocal residence—A wife's residence in the house or village of her husband's kin.

Petroglyphs—Drawings or designs carved or pecked or painted on rock.

Piki—Hopi Indian wafer-thin bread made of ground cornmeal.

Polychrome pottery—Pottery decorated with more than two colors.

Potsherd—A fragment of broken pottery.

Pottery—Jars, bowls, and other vessels made of fired clay.

Projectile point—A term archaeologists use to describe an arrowhead, spearhead, or dart point.

Pueblo—The Spanish word for town, used by archaeologists to refer to certain Southwestern Indians in northern Arizona and New Mexico and their stone and adobe community houses.

Salado—A group of prehistoric Southwestern Indians formerly living in eastern and southern Arizona.

Shaman—The Siberian word for a medicine man.

Sinagua—A group of prehistoric Indians formerly living in the vicinity of Flagstaff, Arizona.

Sipapu—A small hole, generally filled with clean sand, found in the floor of Anasazi kivas and seemingly symbolizing the mythical point where their ancestors emerged from the underworld.

Site—Any place that shows evidence of human occupation, such as houses, pottery, broken stone tools, bones, etc.

Tipi—A Plains Indian hut made of a conical framework of poles covered with skins.

Tribe—A group of people having a common language, often a common name for themselves, definite territory, and a common culture.

Wickiup—A beehive-shaped hut of poles and brush and grass used by many Apache Indians.

Bibliography

AMSDEN, CHARLES A., *Navaho Weaving*. Albuquerque, University of New Mexico Press, 1949.

BAHTI, TOM, *Southwestern Indian Arts and Crafts*. Flagstaff, Arizona, KC Publications, 1964.

BALDWIN, GORDON C., *The Ancient Ones*. New York, W. W. Norton & Company, Inc., 1963.

———— *The Warrior Apaches*. Tucson, Arizona, Dale Stuart King, Publisher, 1965.

———— *How Indians Really Lived*. New York, G. P. Putnam's Sons, 1967.

BUREAU OF INDIAN AFFAIRS, *Indians of Arizona*. Washington, D.C., U.S. Government Printing Office, 1966.

———— *Indians of California*. Washington, D.C., U.S. Government Printing Office, 1966.

———— *Indians of New Mexico*. Washington, D.C., U.S. Government Printing Office, 1966.

———— *American Indian Calendar*. Washington, D.C., U.S. Government Printing Office, 1965.

CAIN, H. THOMAS, *Pima Indian Basketry*. Phoenix, Arizona, The Heard Museum of Anthropology and Primitive Art, 1962.

DOUGLAS, FREDERIC H., and D'HARNONCOURT, RENE, *Indian Art of the United States*. New York, The Museum of Modern Art, 1941.

DUNN, DOROTHY, "America's First Painters." *National Geographic* (March, 1955).

GILPIN, LAURA, *The Pueblos: A Camera Chronicle*. New York, Hastings House, 1941.

HANNUM, ALBERTA, *Spin a Silver Dollar*. New York, The Viking Press, 1945.

KENT, KATE PECK, *The Story of Navaho Weaving*. Phoenix, Arizona, The Heard Museum of Anthropology and Primitive Art, 1961.

KLUCKHOHN, CLYDE, and LEIGHTON, DOROTHEA, *The Navaho*. New York, Doubleday & Company, Inc., 1962.

MCNICHOLS, CHARLES L., *Crazy Weather*. New York, The Macmillan Company, 1944.

MCNITT, FRANK, *The Indian Traders*. Norman, Oklahoma, The University of Oklahoma Press, 1962.

MILLER, JOSEPH, *Arizona Indians*. New York, Hastings House, 1941.

NEWCOMB, FRANC JOHNSON, *Hosteen Klah, Navaho Medicine Man and Sand Painter*. Norman, Oklahoma, The University of Oklahoma Press, 1964.

SIMPSON, RUTH DEETTE, *The Hopi Indians*. Los Angeles, The Southwest Museum, 1953.

SONNICHSEN, C. L., *The Mescalero Apaches*. Norman, Oklahoma, The University of Oklahoma Press, 1958.

SPENCER, ROBERT F., and JENNINGS, JESSE D., *The Native Americans*. New York, Harper & Row, 1965.

STIRLING, M. W., "Indian Tribes of Pueblo Land." *National Geographic* (November, 1940).

———— *Indians of the Americas*. Washington, D.C., The National Geographic Society, 1961.

UNDERHILL, RUTH, *Pueblo Crafts*. Phoenix, Arizona, Phoenix Indian School, 1945.

———— *Work-a-Day Life of the Pueblos*. Phoenix, Arizona, Phoenix Indian School, 1946.

———— *The Papago Indians of Arizona and Their Relatives the Pima*. Lawrence, Kansas, Haskell Institute, 1940.

———— *The Navajos*. Norman, Oklahoma, The University of Oklahoma Press, 1956.

VELARDE, PABLITA, *Old Father, the Story Teller*. Globe, Arizona, Dale Stuart King, Publisher, 1960.

WOODWARD, ARTHUR, *A Brief History of Navajo Silversmithing*. Flagstaff, Arizona, Museum of Northern Arizona, 1938.

Southwestern Museums

Arizona

Arizona State Museum	Tucson
Arizona Pioneers' Historical Society Museum	Tucson
Heard Museum of Anthropology and Primitive Art	Phoenix
Pueblo Grande Museum	Phoenix
Smoki Museum	Prescott
Museum of Northern Arizona	Flagstaff
Navajo Tribal Museum	Window Rock
Fort Verde Museum	Camp Verde
The Amerind Foundation	Dragoon

Colorado

Ute Indian Museum	Montrose
Denver Museum of Natural History	Denver
Denver Art Museum	Denver

New Mexico

Museum of New Mexico	Santa Fe
Museum of Navajo Ceremonial Art	Santa Fe
School of American Research	Santa Fe
Museum of Anthropology, University of New Mexico	Albuquerque
Gallup Museum of Indian Arts and Crafts	Gallup
Coronado State Monument Museum	Bernalillo
Carlsbad Municipal Museum	Carlsbad
Roswell Museum and Art Center	Roswell
Paleo-Indian Institute of Eastern New Mexico , University	Portales
Grand County Museum	Silver City

National Parks and Monuments

The Southwest has more National Parks and Monuments than any other section of the country. Most of these have museums illustrating the prehistoric and historic Indians of that particular area, and many also preserve spectacular Indian ruins that are well worth seeing.

Arizona

Canyon de Chelly National Monument	Chinle
Tonto National Monument	Roosevelt
Navajo National Monument	Tonalea
Casa Grande National Monument	Coolidge
Montezuma Castle National Monument	Camp Verde
Wupatki National Monument	Flagstaff
Walnut Canyon National Monument	Flagstaff
Tuzigoot National Monument	Clarkdale
Chiricahua National Monument	Willcox
Petrified Forest National Park	Holbrook
Grand Canyon National Park	Grand Canyon

Colorado

Mesa Verde National Park	Mesa Verde
Hovenweep National Monument	Cortez

Nevada

Lake Mead National Recreation Area	Boulder City

185

New Mexico

Aztec National Monument	Aztec
Chaco Canyon National Monument	Bloomfield
Bandelier National Monument	Los Alamos
Gran Quivira National Monument	Mountainair
Carlsbad Caverns National Park	Carlsbad
El Morro National Monument	El Morro
Gila Cliff Dwellings National Monument	Silver City

Index

188

go, 152–54; Patayan, 38; Pueblo, 47–48, 151–54; Sinagua, 38; Southern Paiute, 114; Walapai, 114; Western Apache, 152; Zuni, 151
Pueblo Bonito, 9, 43
Pueblo Grande, 9
Pueblo Indians, 42–49, 51–63, 74–92, 141, 142, 144, 145–48, 151–52, 155–58, 160–61, 174, 177; architecture, 43, 76–79; basketry, 142, 144; ceremonies, 89–92; clothing, 80, 147–48; farming, 80–83; hunting, 83–84; kivas, 78–80, 88, 90, 177; political organization, 85; pottery, 47–48, 151–54; religious organization, 87–89; revolt of 1680, 61–62; social organization, 85–87; weaving, 146–48

Quivira, land of, 56

Rio Grande Pueblos, 47, 48, 49, 54, 57, 59, 63, 65, 67, 68, 76, 79, 81, 87, 90, 123
Rituals and ceremonies: Apache, 135–38; Mohave and Yuma, 106–8; Navaho, 133–36; Pima and Papago, 98; Pueblo, 89–92; Walapai and Yavapai, 115

Safford, Arizona, 174
San Carlos Apaches, 173–74
San Gabriel, 57
San Ildefonso Pueblo, 68, 78, 151, 160
San Juan Pueblo, 57, 61, 68
Sand paintings, 134–36
Sandia Pueblo, 67
Santa Clara Pueblo, 68, 76, 151, 160
Santa Fe, 59, 61, 62
Santo Domingo Pueblo, 151, 158
Scaffold House, 9
Shamans and medicine men, 106, 115, 133
Shoshonean language family, 67, 68, 69, 111, 115
Sinagua culture, 38–39, 46, 50
Snake Dance, 90–92
Snaketown, 9, 30
Sosa, Castano de, 57
Southern Paiute Indians, 68, 69, 94, 110–16, 152

Square Tower House, 9
Sunset Crater, 38, 46
Swallow's Nest, 9
Symbolism in Indian art, 140–41

Tanoan language family, 67, 68
Taos Pueblo, 67, 76, 83, 177
Tesuque Pueblo, 68
Tovar, Don Pedro de, 53–54
Tree rings. See Dendrochronology
Tribal government, 167–68
Tucson, Arizona, 63
Tularosa Cave, 29
Tusayan, 53
Tuzigoot Pueblo, 46
Two Raven House, 9
Tyuonyi Pueblo, 48

Ute Indians, 46, 64, 68, 94, 110, 159
Uto-Aztecan language family, 67, 68

Vaca, Cabeza de, 52
Vargas, Diego de, 62
Victorio, 119

Walapai Indians, 38, 64, 65, 69, 94, 110–16, 153
Weaving: Basket Maker, 34–35, 145–46; Hohokam, 146; Hopi, 147–48, 175; Navaho, 148–50, 175; Pueblo, 146–48
Western Apaches, 64, 70, 72, 118–38, 173–74
Window Rock, Arizona, 173
Witchcraft, 106, 131–33

Yaqui Indians, 68
Yavapai Indians, 64, 65, 68, 69, 94, 98, 110–16, 153, 164
Yavapai-Apaches. See Yavapai Indians
Yuma Indians, 64, 65, 68, 69, 93, 94, 98, 101–9, 159
Yuma-Apaches. See Yavapai Indians
Yuman language family, 67, 69, 94, 99, 111

Zia Pueblo, 151, 160
Zuni, 47, 52–54, 64, 65, 66, 75, 76, 77, 79, 81, 84, 85, 86, 87, 89, 90, 127, 151, 155–56, 158, 160, 161, 177
Zunian language family, 67

FROM PUTNAM'S

AMERICAN INDIANS THEN AND NOW is a series under the general editorship of Earl Schenck Miers. It is designed to introduce readers to the principal American Indian tribes as they lived before and after the arrival of the white man.

INDIANS OF THE NORTHERN PLAINS
by William K. Powers

"Carefully researched and organized, stocked with accurate details, this is an entertaining, highly informative account of the American Indians from the northern portion of the region between the Mississippi River and the Rocky Mountains. . . . And the excellent photographs, well placed throughout the book, further heighten the appeal of this fine book."—*School Library Journal* Starred Review

"Parents who respect both historical objectivity and their children's intelligence will introduce them to *Indians of the Northern Plains,* written by a man who knows Indians as well as their history and anthropology. If this is to be a gift and if the giver is capable of such petty dishonesty, he is advised to handle the book carefully and give himself the pleasure and profit of reading it first."—*Book World*

INDIANS OF THE GREAT BASIN AND PLATEAU
by Francis Haines

Among the most interesting Indian tribes in the United States are those of the Great Basin and the Columbia Plateau. Author Francis Haines tells the exciting stories of the Nez Perce, Flatheads, and Shoshoni from earliest times to the present day.

191

The Author

GORDON C. BALDWIN received his PhD in anthropology from the University of Southern California and taught archeology at the universities of Arizona and Omaha. He has excavated prehistoric ruins or been on archeological expeditions in Arizona, New Mexico, Nevada, Utah, Colorado, and Nebraska. The author of numerous scientific articles and several books, Dr. Baldwin lives with his wife in Tucson, Arizona.